RUN LIKE AN ANTELOPE

700 42166 P573

D0954022

pe : on
h /

01/ 08
/ 11

ILL - - 4

GAYLORD MG

RUN LIKE AN ANTELOPE:
On the Road with Phish

Sean Gibbon

THOMAS DUNNE BOOKS/ST. MARTIN'S GRIFFIN
NEW YORK

THOMAS DUNNE BOOKS.
An imprint of St. Martin's Press.

www.stmartins.com

Frontispiece and design by Jane Adele Regina

ISBN 0-312-26330-9

First Edition: February 2001

10 9 8 7 6 5 4 3 2 1

Acknowledgments

Thanks to Jake Elwell for getting this rolling. To Barry Neville, who made it a better book. To Emily Hopkins for seeing it through, and to Elizabeth Catalano for her very good eye. To Shack, Will, Skins, and Dan, who rode along in the Jimmy. To Douglass Titus for his photos. To Arthur Naething for an early vote of confidence. Thanks to David Sleeper, John Paluska, and Sam Ankerson.

And thanks, most of all, to my mom and dad.

Slackers

June 29, Burlington, Vermont

Time to get this thing started. I'm on the road for a month, fol-lowing Phish, living with the fans in campgrounds and motels for the summer tour. Twenty shows in thirty days. The idea is to write from the inside out, the crowd's perspective. The Phish-heads. The traveling cult. The whole scene. The book deal went down in the last week or two and the contract isn't hammered out just yet. My agent assures me everything is in the works. Check's in the mail.

Tomorrow I fly to Kansas, the first show of the summer. Ten-nessee the next night, Atlanta over July 4th, and then a big loop up the coast, winding through Carolina, Virginia, New Jersey, upstate New York, across the border to Canada, and then drop-ping back down into the Midwest at the end of July.

The first thing I needed was a car to pick up in Kansas. The woman at Hertz rattled off some figures, but then later in the afternoon my friend from California called with a good point:

"You can't get a normal rental car," he said. "You'll stick out too much. Think about it. You don't want to pull into the parking lot before the show in a Hertz rental. You need to blend in."

"You're right," I said. "They'll think I'm a narc."

"I'll look up a few things on the Web and get back to you."

He left the number for Rent-A-Wreck on my machine.

I dialed the number.

"I want a car that doesn't look like your average rental car," I said on the phone. "I'm writing this book about all these people who follow this band around the country, and I'm going to travel along with them and I want to, you know, blend in. Have you heard of the band Phish?"

"Ah . . . I think so. Yeah."

"Well, they have lots of fans who follow them everywhere and they drive things like VW buses and Subarus. I don't want a car that looks brand new."

"I hear what you're saying," the guy said.

"So what do you suggest?"

"We got an '88 Buick . . . or how about something like a Chevy Blazer or a Jimmy?"

"Yeah, okay. That sounds good."

"I've got a Jimmy that I've been fixing up. Just put a new engine in it, actually, and I could throw on some new tires for you. Let me tell you, the guys in the shop, we're all stock car racers out here. We know what we're doing."

So tomorrow when I step off the plane in Kansas City, I'm supposed to look out for Kathy in baggage claim. She'll be holding a clipboard with a Rent-A-Wreck sticker on the back.

Philip and I sat on his porch a couple of nights ago drinking beer.

"Watch out for pit bulls," Philip said.

"What?"

"Pit bulls. After the Clifford Ball a few years ago all the Phish-heads came back to Burlington and took over City Park. I swear every one of them had a dog, and nine out of ten were pit bulls. Not even pure breeds, but some Doberman–pit bull cross. The mangiest and meanest-looking dogs you could imagine."

"Jesus."

"And the crowd seems to have more of an edge to it than the old Deadhead crowd," Philip said. "With the Deadheads it was almost self-consciously pacifist, you know. But with this crowd there seems to be more an attitude of I'm-out-for-me-and-mine. I don't know how exactly, I just think it's different."

The next day, another friend called and said, "Four twenty, dude."

"What?"

"Four twenty."

"I don't know what you're talking about."

"You're going on tour and you don't know what four twenty is?"

"Never heard of it."

"Damn, man. It's the code name for marijuana. I think it came from the old police code or something."

"Well, okay, good to know."

"You don't want to get embarrassed out there on the road."

My landlord suggested I get some dreadlocks for the trip. "Oh, it'd be great," she said. "Perfect. You should definitely do it. And they can weave them right into your hair these days."

"Is that right?"

"Oh, yeah. They can. And then you'd have to get pictures. It'd be great. You could do a before-and-after shot for the cover of the book. I love it."

Even if I thought this was a good idea, which I don't, it would never work. With dreadlocks on my head I'd be preoccupied the whole time, arranging them in different styles, scratching, wondering if the disguise was working. I don't think I could meet anyone in the eye with fake dreads. In a million years, I wouldn't introduce myself to a stranger with dreadlocks woven into my scalp.

My girlfriend, Jill, is concerned about the drug scene. Specifically, me taking part in the drug scene. She's a medical student at the University of Vermont here in Burlington.

I know our phone conversations from the road are going to be uncomfortable.

"So what did you do today?" she'll say, thinking to herself, *He's on something, I know it.*

"Oh, not much," I'll say. "Walked around. Did some interviews." And the whole time I'll be thinking, *She doesn't believe me, she thinks I'm tripping.* And the whole time, no matter where I'm calling from, she'll hear some dude beating a drum in the background, which is going to make me sound even more suspicious.

My mom worries about the car situation.

"Rent-A-Wreck?" she said on the phone.

"Yeah, that's just the name, though."

"That sounds *terrible*."

"No, Mom, they're a reputable company. It's just the name. You know, it's their gimmick. Actually, there's a Rent-A-Wreck in every state. It's not just one place in Kansas."

"I think it's *very* unwise."

"It's fine, really. They've put in a new engine."

"A new *engine*! They had to put in a new *engine*?"

"Just to fix it up. They're all stock car racers out there, you know."

"*Stock* car racers?"

"Mom, it's fine. Trust me."

She did get me thinking, though. Why did they put in a new engine? Maybe I should stick with Hertz.

I just need to get this trip started. I feel like I'm on a team that's made the playoffs and I'm sitting around the locker room waiting for the game to begin, thinking too much, wondering what's going to happen.

Last night, Jill and I went out for dinner to this Italian place and we were talking about the trip with the tour itinerary spread across the table when our waiter said, "Hey, I met one of them Phish guys."

"Oh, yeah?" I said. "Which one?"

"One of them Phish guys, you know. I was at this bar and my friend introduces us. He says, 'This is Trey.' And then we're talking and so I say, 'What do you do?' He says, 'I sing.' I'm like, *sing*? So I say, 'What do you sing—*opera*?' He says, 'No, in a band.' And so I say, 'What band?' And he says, 'Phish.' Then I look at him, surprised, and I sip my Bloody Mary and say, 'Okay.'"

Burlington is a small enough town so that everyone—waiters, plumbers, car mechanics—seems to have a Phish story.

"I lived in the same house with the drummer, right down the hall. . . ."

"I did some work on their barn. . . ."

"What's-his-name comes in to get his hair cut. . . ."

"I used to party with those guys. . . ."

My own Phish story is that I've taught squash to Page McConnell, the keyboardist, at a local fitness club. Which was pretty cool. He said it was the first time he'd exercised regularly in fifteen years, what with the constant touring. One time I called his house to change a lesson time and his wife said, "Hold on a second." It was quiet in the background when she called his name and then I heard what sounded like a door opening and then all of a sudden the loudest music you can imagine came blasting into the phone for a few seconds, pure noise, like an explosion. He must have been in the music room.

Phish are Vermont's celebrities. Our celebrities. Even though most people in America have never even heard of Phish, everyone in Vermont has heard of them and everyone thinks they're huge—real live stars. Who else do we have to boast about? Whenever something with Phish happens, it makes its way around town. A week or so ago, Jim Carrey, in Vermont for a movie shoot, sang a few songs with the band at Trey's barn. They sang a couple of Beatles tunes together, and supposedly Carrey's voice isn't that bad and when he didn't know the lyrics he was able to invent some of his own.

The other night I saw Trey and Page sit in with a blues band at a local bar. They came on stage unannounced and there were maybe a hundred people in the room. It was one of those perfect Saturday nights—warm air blowing in the window, no line for beer, perfect sight lines, great music. In a way, Phish is still a Burlington band. Last year they grossed over $23 million in ticket sales and played all over the world, including Amsterdam and Barcelona, and yet between tours they are still part of the local music scene, each of them popping up here and there with different bands.

You can find a halfway decent band somewhere in town most nights, with plenty of people turning up for the shows even on like a Tuesday night. College kids come out by the hundreds. They travel in packs. And you'll always spot some scattered middle-aged couples with long ponytails dancing in the corner. But the most common type, the most recognizable guy out at the bars on your average night, is the Burlington Dude: a twenty-or-thirty-something guy with longish hair, a week-long beard—often some sort of writer, artist, musician who makes money waiting tables, bartending, landscaping, etc. . . . Basically a slacker. A dropout. "We're hoping he'll go to law school some-day," his parents are saying back home in Connecticut. "But he's up there in Burlington doing who knows what."

When I first moved to Burlington a few years ago, I lived in a first-floor apartment of a three-story brick house, directly beneath a guy learning to play the bongos. He was this little dude from Long Island, maybe twenty-one or twenty-two, with long dreadlocks and scraggly hair on his cheeks, who woke up about noon and stood in the front yard smoking cigarettes, looking very pale and out of it. The bongo routine started up at approximately two in the morning. Thump, thump, thump. He was terrible. Had no idea how to play. In the afternoons, he cranked Bob Marley out of his window and stepped outside to walk his dog, a skinny mutt named Marley who crapped all over the lawn and occasionally got hit by cars on the busy street.

The whole thing didn't bother me much, bongos and all. I sort of adjusted to his routine—stayed up with the bongos, slept late, ate breakfast at noon watching him through the window with his cigarette. (One bonus to living among slackers: they're always blasting music or shouting out the window or drinking beers on the ratty front-porch couch, so if you are a procrastinator, like me, then you always have an excuse not to get down to business . . . How can I write with the goddamn bongos? Might as well watch MTV.)

One morning I was sitting there eating breakfast when a brown liquid dripped from the ceiling right into the center of my kitchen table. I called the landlord, expecting the worst, and he went upstairs to investigate. He came down a few minutes later and explained that there was a bong spill last night, not to worry, that the brown liquid on my table was simply a bit of bong juice which had trickled through the cracks in the wood floor above. The landlord was a pothead, too.

It's a town full of potheads. Underachievers. It's amazing anything gets done around here. I don't mean this in a negative way. I love slackers. I feel much better surrounded by them. I mean, if I rise and shine in the a.m. and have at least some semblance of a career, well, then I'm way ahead of your average twenty-something in Burlington. People here put off career decisions and future plans and just hang out, skateboarding and washing dishes, smoking pot, checking out a band on a Tuesday night. One of the most popular bumper stickers around town, often spotted on rusty bumpers of old Subarus, is the Ben & Jerry's slogan: "If it's not fun, why do it?"

There is of course a yuppie element in Burlington, like you'll find in most college towns: nice restaurants, boutiques, Banana Republic, and all that. But the overall feeling of Burlington is more—what?—crunchy, skateboardy . . . bongy. Like there's this one pizza joint on Main Street, Mr. Mike's, that gets a lot of the late-night bar crowd. I swear everyone that works there is high for their shift. Usually a Grateful Dead bootleg blasts from the stereo and a tie-dyed waitress floats around the place, wandering with a pie on her shoulder trying to remember who ordered the large sausage and pepperoni. The tables are always sprinkled with that gritty pizza-crust stuff that sticks to your fingers. I've had some of the best and worst pizza in that place. You never know what you'll get. But I keep going back.

There's a bar in town called Three Needs which is definitely part
of the scene—dreadlocked dudes mixed in with the seven-year-
plan college students, a Phish song on the stereo, everyone seeming to know each other even on a busy night. John McIlwaine
used to work at Three Needs and now he just goes to hang out.
He's been to hundreds of Phish shows—so many he can't keep
track and rolls his eyes when you ask how many. He looks like a
lot of guys in town—messy brown hair, unshaven, t-shirt, jeans,
a knit hat. He's from New Jersey, which if you take New York,
New Jersey, and Connecticut then you'll account for about 90
percent of the Burlington scene. John likes the summer tour least
of all the tours. "It's a rowdy party, the summer crowd," he said at
Three Needs. "There's a lot of people that just go and get fucked
up, you know. A lot of drunk frat kids. It's a big party. It's the closest thing to running away and joining the circus. But it's tough
because you don't have people who are really focusing on the
music. But that's a big generalization. Summer tour's just a lot
different. So much of the scene is really in the parking lot because
it's warm. You're not freezing your ass off. You can pretty much
hang out in the sun all day drinking beers getting retarded. That's
sort of the summer vibe. A lot of people on the lawn getting really
fucked up. A lot of kids on the ground afterwards."

McIlwaine, or "Johnny Mac," is a serious Phish fan who can
tell you just about anything about the band—nights they were
on, nights they were off, nights they reached new highs. He's followed them through Europe, even once rode a ferry from Alaska
for a run of California shows. "I've seen these guys in tiny little
shithole rooms, you know. I never thought these guys would be
as big as they are. It's funny, I'd give tapes to everybody I met,
but I always thought nobody would ever get it. I was living in
Alaska when they sold out the Beacon Theater and I laughed. I
read it on the Net and I just laughed. No *fucking* way. That's
hilarious. And then I'm seeing them at the Garden on the thirti-
eth, you know. And that was unbelievable—Madison Square
Garden sold out."

Johnny Mac is typical of a certain type of diehard music fan—
extremely smart, totally obsessed with music, with an uncanny
memory for shows years ago and a record collection at home that
is worth more than anything else he owns. He seems to think of
everything in terms of music, and when he talks it's a bit like listening to jazz—he's all over the place, sometimes mixed up and
turned around, and other times you think, *My God, he's got it
exactly right.* He'll quote Goethe or Thomas Mann and you
think to yourself, *What the hell?* . . . but he moves fast, never
stays with one thought for more than a few seconds, and he'll
leave Goethe for a description of John Coltrane that grabs you by
the collar with its inventiveness.

Like a lot of serious fans, Johnny Mac is very critical of the
band. Part of the appeal of a Phish show is watching the puzzle
come together, hearing the musicians work it out, improvise,
stretch, come together. The really big moments don't happen
every night. "I've gone for a long time," he said, "so I've got
really high standards. I'm constantly disappointed. But when
they break through it's always for me a big big big moment. It's
like a tightwire act. You're seeing them to see if they make it.
When they make it, it's great."

One of these moments, according to Johnny Mac, came in
Europe a couple of years ago in a small town in Italy. It happened
during a song called "Fluffhead."

"It was great. All of a sudden they're up there and it was like
they sold themselves on it. All of a sudden they *believed* in
'Fluffhead.' It was like they were young again, like being in
Rhode Island and seeing them at—what's that, the Campus
Club?—where they did all that 'Follow the Yellow Brick Road'
and shit. They *believed* in 'Fluffhead,' and I mean they just
played the shit out of it. It was triumphant. It was such an utter
moment of absolute bliss for me. I was ripped, but I mean honestly there was such . . . you know, I started crying during 'Fluffhead.' This is perfect. It was that moment where all of a sudden
everything was perfect."

It's this kind of peak that, in part, makes a person follow a band across the Atlantic. And it's this kind of peak that has made Phish unbelievably successful. But still it's strange, the whole phenomenon, the whole business of packing up and following a band wherever they go. It's weird. Fanatical. All these people wandering around, following a band to Ohio and Oregon, back and forth across country, passing their days on the road, hanging out in parking lots, cooking on a grill, listening to tapes, taking drugs, dancing around their vans.

And yet there is something incredibly romantic about it all. Almost irresistible. The call of the road. Jack Kerouac. *Easy Rider.* The Grateful Dead. For whatever reason, Phish is the last place for this sort of thing in America today, the last frontier.

Organic Lemonade

June 30, Bonner Springs, Kansas

Flying somewhere over the Midwest on an overcrowded flight, knocking knees with the person sitting across from me, who munches some peanuts and reads his newspaper. Cute blond girl to my left seems annoyed that I'm pecking away on my laptop and whenever she looks over to see what I'm doing, I scroll down so she can't read the screen. Screw it. I got to write this sucker. Couple thousand words a day is what I'm aiming for. Crank it out.

Initially, I had planned to camp each night after the show, really go for the whole immersion thing. "Oh, yeah," I told my friends a week ago, "I'll be camping each night. That's part of the idea, you know, really go for it." But then, a few days before the trip, I panicked and called up every Best Western and Motel 6 along my route and booked a room for each night of the tour. I figure I'll camp at some point for the experience, but I'll put it off as long as possible. I'll do just about anything to avoid camping. Can't stand it. I've been maybe three or four times, all disasters. When I bought my tent the other day, it put me in a terrible mood. "I need the cheapest thing you got," I said to the EMS sales clerk. "I'll only be using it this summer and never again." It cost me eighty bucks.

So. The first day of the summer tour. I have that feeling where you're excited about something but you're not sure exactly what. I haven't seen Phish since New Year's Eve and I'm psyched for tonight's show. I keep thinking of walking into the venue with the band on stage and tens of thousands of people fired up, ready to go. There's nothing like it.

A few minutes ago, in a Chicago airport restaurant, a red-headed guy with a box of fruit pulled up a chair at the next table. Clearly a Phishhead. Hemp necklace, old t-shirt, overstuffed backpack, and the box of fruit was a giveaway—something to sell on tour for gas and ticket money.

"Are you going to the show tonight?" I said.

"Not tonight. I'm joining up in Atlanta."

"How much are you doing?"

"Whole thing, man. I'll end up back here. This is my drop-off."

"Maybe I'll see you out there," I said. "I'm doing it all, too."

"Right on," he said. "You'll *definitely* see me around."

Have you seen the show Fanatic on MTV? It starts with a contest: Send us a videotape explaining why you would like to meet Ricky Martin or the Backstreet Boys or whoever, and if we choose you we'll show up, completely unannounced, whisk you away to the airport and fly you off to meet your favorite star, up close, in person. It's one of those shows I can't stop watching once I tune in. At the start of the show, when they surprise the Fanatic, usually a teenage boy or girl standing beside a high-school locker, I always think, *How pathetic*. But then, somehow, as the Fanatic goes to the airport, walks through the terminal, fidgets in the limo and talks about how nervous she is, my attitude changes. I end up rooting for the Fanatic. "Settle down," I say to the screen. "Don't screw this up." I always end up liking the Fanatic, no matter how corny her questions.

Fanatics—and by this I mean all serious fans, diehards—are usually pretty likeable people. Interesting to be around, at least in a crowd. Even if it's a big fat guy at an ice hockey game cursing the ref and swilling beer—well, at least he's pumped up, totally involved. There's something very unselfish about being a diehard fan, committing all your attention and focus onto someone else. And of course fanatics have been around forever. Think of the old black-and-white reels of the Beatles stepping off the plane to the screaming girls. Last summer at a Phish show, I spotted this blond dreadlocked kid in the front row. Maybe nineteen or twenty. He had waited there all day under a blazing sun to claim his front-row spot, and when the band came on he just stood there, mouth open, staring at them for the longest time, hardly moving.

In an hour, when the plane lands in Kansas City, I meet my college buddy Shack, who's flying from the East Coast on a separate flight. He's coming along for the first leg of the trip. I'm not going to mention his full name or where he works because he said on the phone he's worried about his company's drug-testing policy. He was hired about a year ago and doesn't know what the policy is exactly. And he likes this job a hell of a lot more than grad school. (In his spare time, he struggles with a master's English thesis which many never get written. "I had to read *Moby Dick* twice," Shack said. "The whole thing. I hated that fucking book." He said he would bring his laptop along for the trip and maybe get some work done. Some books, too.)

When I told him that we'd be traveling through the South, the first thing he said was, "*Oooh* . . . southern girls." Shack is a stud. He looks like a young John Travolta, the one from *Saturday Night Fever*. Like Travolta, he's got a certain swagger and charm. Women love him. I'm sure he's flirting with some stewardess out there in the sky right now. "Excuse me, ma'am? Hello, I was wondering. . . ."

Shack has been to a bunch of Dead shows, but like a lot of old Grateful Dead fans, he hasn't seen a Phish show. Which is strange, because in many ways Phish has picked up where the Grateful Dead left off when Jerry Garcia died in 1995. They have a unique and fanatical tribe of fans that drop out of society and travel to all the shows. The sixties counterculture of LSD and rock and roll—kept alive by the Deadheads well into the 1990s—has been passed on to the next generation. Phishheads even dress like hippies: flowery dresses, dreadlocked hair, scruffy beards, moccasins, tie-dyed T-shirts. Phish is carrying the torch, keeping

the party going. But not with the same fans. Among many Deadheads there is a general suspicion of Phish and Phishheads. One
of my best friends, a Deadhead from Santa Cruz who spent years
on the road, can't believe that I listen to Phish. He thinks it's
ridiculous. He won't even give them a try. Part of it is the age factor. Deadheads are older and Phishheads are younger. But it's
more than that. The Dead truly captured a time, an era: the sexual revolution, the emerging drug culture, the war protests. They
came out of San Francisco in the sixties, and that spirit or vibe or
whatever you want to call it lingered with the band for thirty
years. Phish is not connected to anything like that. Four college
kids met in Vermont in the 1980s and started playing the local
bars. There wasn't anything to protest, there wasn't any cultural
revolution. So they wrote songs about dragons and princes and
characters named Sloth and Lawn Boy. The lyrics really didn't
make sense. They didn't mean anything. The songs were whimsi-
cal and funny, even goofy. They sounded great and the music carried the words along. If Phish embodies something about their
times, it's that things are rolling along pretty well and let's enjoy
it while we can.

"I don't want to be the oldest one on tour," Shack said on the phone.

"Don't worry. There will be plenty of people our age."

I'm twenty-seven years old. A strange age: Still close enough to my college days but also staring down the barrel at thirty. Caught in the middle. Perfect time for a road trip.

"I haven't been to a concert in four years," Shack said. "Last time was at a Dead show at Giants Stadium and some fat chick fell off the second story. Do you remember that?"

"Sort of. I think I remember hearing about it."

"It was like something out of *The Naked Gun.*"

"What happened to her?"

"Oh, she was fine. But she crushed, I mean crushed, a couple of guys she fell on. It was in our section, and we had like twenty people around us shrooming and they freaked out. They were like, 'We gotta leave,' and they just took off."

Kathy from Rent-A-Wreck picks us up from the airport in a big Ford Explorer. Very professional and organized with the clipboard. This bodes well for our rental.

"We're in Kansas—yeeeee-haw!" Shack says as he climbs into the backseat.

Kathy glances in her rearview.

"Oh . . ." Shack says. "I'm not suggesting that you say 'yee-haw' in Kansas. I'm just saying it for myself, you know."

"That's fine," Kathy says. "What's the name of the band again?"

"Phish," I say.

"With a P-H!" Shack chimes in from the back.

I turn around in my seat and give him the pipe-down look.

"And you're going to be following them around and writing about it?" Kathy says.

"Yeah. You see they've got all these fans that are really, well, into it. They travel from show to show. It's kind of a cult thing. Part of the idea for the book is that Americans are fascinated by cults of any kind, you know."

"Sort of like that whole Kool-Aid cult?" Kathy says.

"You mean the acid tests?"

Kathy flicks her eyes sideways, with a hint of concern. *Who are these people?* "No," she says. "I'm talking about that cult where they drank all that Kool-Aid to commit suicide."

"Oh," I say. "Yeah. Well, um . . . kind of a different thing here."

After a long discussion about Scientology (Kathy is a believer), we pull into Rent-A-Wreck and meet Richard, the owner of the garage, a big guy in his fifties with a giant belly. He walks us out to the Jimmy, which looks pretty good with the new tires.

"Hell, I wish I was going on this trip," he says. "I'm jealous. I went to the original Woodstock. Didn't actually make it to the concert, though, because of the traffic. It was backed up for miles. Sat there for a while and turned around."

"Is that right?"

"Sure did. When you called up, I knew this was the car for the trip. I knew right away. You see, the back comes down like this and you could stick a keg right back there."

"All *right*," Shack says.

"Oh, yeah," Richard says, "you guys will have a great time. Plus, she's got a new engine that runs nice and a new set of tires. You guys will have a great time."

An hour before the show, after a trip to Kmart for an extra-large cooler and a Nerf football, we park the Jimmy outside the Sandstone Amphitheatre, crack open a few beers, and stand in the pouring rain. Thunder rolls across the sky with zaps of purple lightning.

"We're in fucking Kansas and it's raining," Shack says. "Pouring rain. The goddamn dust bowl. I got *The Grapes of Wrath* in the back of the car for chrissake."

We crank up Jimmy Cliff's *The Harder they Come* and watch a young couple kissing in the rain . . . *Pressure gonna drop on you* . . . They're really going for it. Not just one kiss for a few seconds. She digs her nails into his back. He grabs her long hair in a fist, twists it. They last for at least two minutes, paying no attention to the lightning streaking around them. Then they stop, drink some beer, and kiss some more. After a big clap of thunder, we jump back into the car and swipe the windshield clear on the inside so we can keep watching. Something about the rain makes people horny. I swear, every time it rains at a concert people start mugging.

Two guys from Nebraska wander over this way, drenched. They spot our big blue cooler sticking out the back and ask for a couple of beers.

"Is Phish big in Nebraska?" I say.

"Yeah, pretty big." The one with the beard nods and wipes his glasses. "We're from Lincoln, which is a college town. So they're pretty big there. Hey, you guys got any pot?"

"No," Shack says. "But tell us if you find any."

"Right on," they say and head off in the rain. "Thanks for the beer."

"They'll never find any weed," Shack says. "Look at them. *Nebraska?* No way."

"Especially with this crowd. It's kind of mellow compared to your average parking-lot scene. Not many dealers. Very midwestern."

Normally, there is a staggering amount of commerce in the parking lot before the show. Thousands and thousands of dollars in crumpled bills change hands. You can buy just about anything. Food, particularly vegetarian stuff like burritos and grilled cheese. Beer, usually top-shelf bottles like Sammy Smith and Sierra Nevada. Clothes, mostly tie-dyes and long hippie dresses, and all sorts of beads, necklaces, bracelets, rings. And of course drugs: pot, mushrooms, acid are the big three, followed by Ecstasy, which seems to be gaining ground quickly.

But the rain here has squashed business this evening. It's coming down hard, in big bullet-sized drops that ricochet off the Jimmy's hood. Lightning slashes the horizon and I wonder if the show will be canceled. There's no roof above the Sandstone

Amphitheatre and I think that thousands of sweaty Phishheads dancing on a wide-open lawn might provide a good target for a bolt or two.

We have an extra ticket for tonight's show, and as the rain lets up for a moment Shack takes off to try and sell it. He quickly starts negotiations with a scraggly-haired little barefoot guy with a patchy beard and no shirt. Like a lot of Phishheads, this guy looks a little bit like Shaggy from *Scooby-Doo*. I walk over to see what's happening.

"I don't have any money, man," Shaggy says.

"None?" Shack says.

"Un-uh."

"How about some pot?"

He reaches into his pockets and comes up empty-handed. "No, man." He looks to be in his early twenties, super-skinny, with long arms, big elbows, and a chest that's sort of caved in. His belly protrudes in a malnourished kind of way. He probably weighs about 120.

"What do you got?" Shack says.

"Garlic grilled cheese, man. I could hook you up with a couple of sandwiches."

Shack looks at the little man and then at me. "What do you think?"

"Well," I say—Shaggy noticing me for the first time—"okay. Fine. Let's do it."

"I've got some organic lemonade, too, man," he says, leading us back to his yellow school bus painted with odd streaks of blue and red and orange. Dirty curtains cover the windows.

"You're a sucker," Shack hisses, shaking his head. "I'm never selling anything with you again."

Our man disappears inside the bus. Mangy gray dogs skulk around the big tires, sniffing the ground. A skinny woman with a microphone marches up and down the steps of the school bus, announcing over and over, "Garlic grilled cheese. That's right. We got garlic grilled cheese. Only a dollar. One dollar." The mike doesn't make her voice any louder. It just makes it scratchy-sounding. In general, electronics in the parking lot are terrible. Car stereos are old and blown out. Boom boxes on top of cars are like ten years old, and when you throw a Phish bootleg in there and twist the volume up all the way (which everyone does), the music sounds like a clanking washing machine.

I pass on the organic lemonade, a toxic shade of brown in a murky plastic bottle. Our new friend is happy to have this ticket and he skips around after handing over the grilled cheese. Scoring a ticket for free is called "getting miracled," as in "I got miracled tonight." On any particular night, there may be a thousand people in the parking lot looking for a miracle: "I need a miracle," "Who's got my miracle?" A lot of fans, like Shaggy, with literally no cash flow, come on tour with an empty wallet and hope to start a pile of greasy dollar bills from grilled cheese sales—enough money to buy a ticket for the next show.

The sandwiches aren't very good. We take a bite or two and head into the show. It's always interesting going to a Phish show with someone new. Shack can't believe Mike Gordon's hair. Gordon, the bassist, has a head of hair that is sort of a mix between a mop and an Afro. It's not that long, but it sprouts out the sides and on top with incredible volume.

"Look at that hair," Shack says. "It's fucking great. He looks like someone out of, I don't know, Foreigner. He's great. And he just stands there like a board. Look at him."

"I see him."

"And so the drummer, he wears a dress every show?"

"Just about," I say. "Every show I've been to."

"Does he have a wife and kids?"

Jon Fishman, the drummer, wears a dress on stage. It's a gray shapeless thing with red circles on it. He's had it for years and it's pretty threadbare. He's a short guy with a beard who always looks like he just rolled out of bed. Once in a while, he gets off his stool and runs around the stage like a wild boar, then hides behind his drum set peering out into the darkness, and then charges out again, waving his arms above his head. On occasion, he lifts his dress for the audience.

After a few minutes, Shack dances around with everyone else, immediately drawn in by the music. It's hard to describe Phish's music. I'm not a music critic and don't plan to write a nightly review of their songs. If you haven't been to a Phish show before, all I can say is, Go as soon as you can. If you've been to shows, you know that sometimes they're really good, sometimes a bit off, and sometimes they're out of this world. Some of their songs are short and simple, with a slow-building steady melody and a harmony that could work as a lullaby. Other songs last twenty minutes and wander off to who knows where. Phish tunes are bluesy, funky, bluegrassy, and mostly just good old rock and roll driven by Trey Anastasio's electric guitar. If one of the measures of a great guitar player is creating your own distinctive sound, Trey has done just that. You can recognize his guitar anywhere.

All the songs make you dance. Phish is the best live rock and roll band in the country right now, with no sign of slowing down. They'll only get bigger. And their traveling fans—this massive group of preppies and dropouts and stoners and misfits—well, there's nothing else in America quite like it. No other band, no other sports team, inspires this kind of fanaticism or loyalty.*

Sam Ankerson works in the management office for Strangefolk, another Burlington band, and he says that without question Phish is king of the hill for all the other jam bands in the country.

"Phish didn't invent jam music but they've invented the current formula for it," he said, "which is much more multi-genre than the Grateful Dead ever were. Combining every conceivable sort of music. Sort of an irreverence for lyrics, which bums me out at times, but also was one of the main reasons that the door

---

*One night, after the summer tour was over, I was sitting in a sushi bar on Nantucket and got talking for a while with a stranger. When I asked him if he had heard of the band Phish, he looked over and said, "Phish? Sure. It's not a band, it's a movement."

got open for a lot of other jam bands. When the Grateful Dead were playing, there were no other jam bands. Not nearly like the legions of jam bands the way there are now. A lot of that was just because the Dead had such a grip on everyone's imagination, but also, you know, that was the model and that's fucking hard—to not only write amazing songs but also have sick lyrics. But Phish, with a sense of humor, sort of threw lyrics out the window, took that piece of the puzzle out. Really what they do better than what anyone ever has is hit the peak, coming back with this three-chord slamming thing and then waaaaaa, all the lights come on and the place goes absolutely mental. Now it seems really simple and that's what every single jam band does. They all have different little things they do, but then everyone winds up doing the peak. And that's why we can all survive, because everyone loves the peak. Literally every jam band you can think of incorporates the whole guitar-driven peak. With some guitarists it's really kind of ugly how much they imitate Trey."

Like the thirty or so successful jam bands that tour clubs around the U.S.—MOE, String Cheese Incident, Disco Biscuits, Deep Banana Blackout, Medeski Martin & Wood are a few—like these bands, Strangefolk is able to eke out a living constantly touring, occasionally selling out small clubs in places like New York, Colorado, San Francisco. The problem for Strangefolk and all of these other jam bands comes down to one thing: Phish.

"We get hammered when they're even in the same half of the country," Sam said. "Everyone does, dude. I swear to God. We get this touring-industry book called *Pole Star* which has everyone's tour in it. You'll see Phish's tour and you look at every other jam band, we're all on the other side of the country. If you think about it, when all these bands started getting some juice, started getting some steam, Phish was in Europe for two years. And that's when all these bands either made a jump or flat out got started. And everyone's sort of plateaued off now that Phish is back on tour.

"There's basically two ways of making it. You can either be an

artist who just makes hit albums, perennially, whatever—The
Red Hot Chili Peppers. Or you're a band that lives its life on the
road. A lot fewer of those. The Grateful Dead, Phish. The reason
there aren't more is there's only room for one or two of those at
a given time, because there are only so many people in the world
who are willing to be so fanatical about a band that they're going
to follow them all over the place."

Midway through the first set, Shack becomes mesmerized by
a woman dancing behind us with long black hair and silver
sparkles on her cheeks and a sexy smile. He keeps turning around
and telling me to check her out. She is beautiful. For a Phishhead
to look that good, in baggy clothes and tangled hair, she really
must be beautiful—no makeup or stylish clothes to help her out.
And she's wearing this shirt that a lot of women on tour wear:
the front has different designs patched together in squares, like a
quilt, and the back is just a piece of string tied like a shoelace. It
may sound like a sexy top, but it's not. Kind of goofy. It looks sort
of like a smock.

Even though it's only the first night of the summer tour, a film
of slime covers everyone here, dust and sweat and smoke and
beer. It's only going to get worse. I can feel the grime on my skin,
slippery and sticky. I'm glad I'm not camping tonight in the rain
and mud. We've already checked into the Best Western and we
left the air conditioner running.

After the show we sit in our seats for a while, waiting for the
place to clear out.

"Wait here," Shack says, and takes off. A minute later he
appears up on stage, jumping up and down in his flip-flops, calling out "Wooooooo-hoo!" to an empty amphitheater. Then he
does a little dance.

In the parking lot, we toss the football under the lights. One of
those nasty dogs comes out of nowhere and steals it from Shack
and darts away with it in his drooling jaws. I think I recognize the
gray mutt from the grilled-cheese bus, but I can't say for sure

because they all look the same, especially in the dark—small, striped like a tiger, bristly-haired, droopy-eared, panting, always panting.

We chase it for a while.

"What's up with all these dogs?" Shack says.

"I know. They're everywhere. It's like a separate breed on tour."

"Ugliest mutts I've ever seen." Shack grabs for the ball. "They must all hump other Phish dogs."

Not as Bad as Ozzy

July 1, Nashville, Tennessee

Driving along I-70 to Nashville. Illinois is an ugly state. I tend to group all the midwestern states together, but the landscapes vary, and they all seem to be better than this—nothing to look at. Not even farmland. At least in Iowa you have the corn, in Kansas the awesome flatness and the huge sky.

Shack is driving and drinking a V-8 juice. We just ate at Wendy's for the second time in three meals. "You can eat and drink whatever you want as long as you have a V-8 everyday," he says.

I'm looking at a map, trying to find a better route to Nashville. There isn't one.

"We're just going for it," Shack says. "On the road. I can see how you could get used to this life, you know. No worries about money. No job. No fucking phone calls. It's a life without consequences."

We pull into a gas station and a group of girls in a red Honda, hands and bare feet sticking out the windows, wave to us and call out something, peeling back onto the steaming highway.

"Did you see that?" Shack says. "That just made my day. They waved to us. I *love* that! Did you see that?"

As the sun sets, a nasty storm whips up over this terrible land and pounds the car with rain and thunder, flashing the highway with bursts of lightning. I'm driving now, and Shack blasts the CD player, singing along. Some more Jimmy Cliff, which seems to be the soundtrack for our trip . . . *You can get it if you really*

want/You can get it if you really want . . . The driving is terrible
and my nerves are a bit raw.

"Do you want some water?" Shack says.

"No."

"Do you want a beer?"

"No."

"How about a Snickers?"

"No. Shut up. I'm trying to concentrate."

"How about some nachos and salsa? A little dip might be
nice?"

"Stop it."

"You're way too nervous. You gotta settle down—hey! stay to
the right. You're swerving. Just watch the white line along the
shoulder."

"Okay, okay."

"On a scale of one to ten, how nervous are you?"

"I don't know. Shut up. About a five. This fucking rain and the
wind. I've never seen anything like this."

"I'd say you're about a six."

"Yeah, well, maybe I'm a six. I think I'm going to pull over."

"Bad idea, dude. Dangerous. No one will see you. Just keep
going."

After a few hours of this, Nashville appears on the horizon. It's
ten o'clock and we've missed the show.

"It's no big deal, baby," Shack says, switching into his
Swingers mode. "We'll go into Nashville, get a couple of cowboy
hats and go for it."

"Sounds like a plan."

"We'll see if they know about Phish. You can do some interviews."

"I'm not—"

"I'm going to shower, shave, and get some Nashville ass, baby.
Time to get our shwerve on."

I'm not sure where the phrase "get your shwerve on" comes
from. Shack may have invented it. He says it all the time. Basi-

cally, it means "time to rally" or "time to get things rolling."
Have you seen the movie *Swingers*? Shack's idol is Vince
Vaughn. He quotes his lines all the time and I think this may be
one of them.

The woman behind the desk at the Best Western seems a bit
frantic.
"I don't see your name here on the list," she says. "And we are
sold out tonight, sir."
"I called a week ago and made a reservation."
"I'm sorry, sir, but I don't have your name. Did you call the
800 number? We do have problems with that sometimes. . . .
Wait—oh, yes, here it is on this list. I found it. Sorry, we're very
busy tonight." She shuffles some papers while a young boy in an
arm cast tugs at her sleeve, asking if he can please go for a swim.
"Expecting a big crowd?" I say.
"Oh, yes. All the Phish people are here. They'll be coming back
from the concert pretty soon."
"What will that be like?"
"Not as bad as Ozzy Osbourne and not as mellow as Shania
Twain."
"How bad was Ozzy?"
"Let's just say we have a few lawsuits because of it. The police
were here."
"What happened?"
"Oh, it was just crazy."
"What did they do? I mean, did they throw chairs through the
windows?"
At this point she glances up from her computer, suspiciously.
Who is this guy? Too many questions. Maybe he's from insur-
ance, undercover here to investigate the Ozzy report . . .
"I don't really remember," she says, pushing the room key
over the counter.
This is a problem with writing a book: you want to ask ques-
tions, you need to ask questions, but not everybody likes ques-

tions. Most people don't go around asking gas attendants, hotel clerks, waiters, policemen a series of questions about things. You can usually get away with three or four. More than five questions, people start getting suspicious.

The cowboy hats and the Nashville scene doesn't happen. The storm rages on. We stand outside our room on the second floor drinking Coronas from the bottle without limes, wondering how late the bars in Nashville stay open on a Thursday night. Across the parking lot, the pool appears black in the yellow haze of the storm.

"We do not have our shwerve on," Shack says.

"No we don't."

"Tough with the weather."

"Yeah," I say. "At least we're not camping."

The parking lot starts to fill up with Phishheads coming back from the show. A Volkswagen bus pulls in and three people dash out the side door into the rain, howling. The Best Western Phishhead crew is generally pretty upscale. These are college kids with their parents' credit cards or people in their twenties with real jobs, coming on tour for a few days. Plenty of Subarus and Jettas. Even a few Saabs. A Best Western room costs about sixty bucks a night. The Phishheads selling grilled cheese don't have this kind of cash. They're back at the campground, pitching a tent in the downpour or curled up inside a bus or maybe marching around the campsite barefoot in the dark with a greasy napkin full of sandwiches, looking to make some more money.

Up on the second-floor balcony we hang out with two guys who just came back from the show. "It was bad ass," one of them says. "They had these local bluegrass guys come on stage with banjos. The rain was pretty bad and it was stinging after a while. But it was bad ass. We heard a great 'Punch You in the Eye,' a killer 'Icculus-Divided Sky.'" These guys, both nineteen, are from Virginia and they play in a band together, whose name I didn't quite get . . . Fusion something. They're on tour for about a week.

"So what kind of music do you guys play?" I say.

"Different stuff, you know. We jam. We have some of our own songs and we do some old stuff, too."

"Who do you listen to?"

"We listen to Phish . . . and, like, the Dead, Hendrix, Zeppelin."

"How about bands today—anyone you like?"

They both look at each other blankly.

"Um . . . we don't . . . let's see . . . You mean like modern bands? . . . No one, really. Actually, Kravitz. We listen to Lenny Kravitz."

If you had to put together a profile of the typical nineteen-year-old male Phishhead, a year out of high school and doing the tour, it would look something like this: On the small side, skinny, usually shirtless and quite pale. Shoulder-length hair, kind of greasy and stringy. Not a jock or a nerd. More like the cool quiet kid, kind of distant, hanging out in the back of the classroom. Considered by other kids to be a burnout, a band guy. Smart but doesn't study much. Or maybe he's into philosophy. He's the one smoking pot before everyone else, before he's even kissed a girl. A junior-high stoner. Probably has an older brother also into Phish or the Dead.

We smoke up with the Virginia guys and watch the rain.

"I started going to Grateful Dead shows with my dad," the one with the hemp necklace says. "He'd take me along. It was great. That's how I got started. He's doesn't go to the Phish shows."

"So you guys going to college?" Shack says.

"Maybe. Haven't decided yet."

"You got some options?"

"Yeah, I got options. I don't have to go."

Back in the room, Shack jumps out of bed. "What the hell is that!" he says, pointing at a moth beside the lamp.

PHOTO COURTESY OF DOUGLASS M. TITUS

"It's just a moth."

"No, it's not. Fuck that! Look at the size of it! Look at its things."

"Settle down. It'll fly out if you leave the door open."

"I don't like anything with larvae."

"I don't see any larvae. Just leave it alone."

The moth tears around the room. Shack swipes at it from about ten feet away and retreats to the bathroom howling about cocoons. It is a big sucker, with wiry antennae and a head that you can actually see. After it flies out the open door, back into the storm, Shack bolts the lock and sits down on his bed.

"Did you see the size of that thing?" he says, wrapping the covers tight.

We stay up until three a.m. watching a terrible movie on Showtime about this woman who gets abducted by aliens and then has the power to zap people back on earth with laser-beam eyes before sucking their blood. Between kills she walks around asking all these very basic questions about everyday life because the aliens stole her memory and she doesn't know how to do the simplest things, like use a fork.

"It's like *Splash*," Shack says. "You know how in *Splash* where she gets all her knowledge as she goes along."

"What are you talking about?"

"The mermaid in *Splash*. She doesn't know anything and has to pick up things as she goes along."

The Green Potion

July 2, Jack Daniel's Country

Late breakfast at the Waffle House, trying to jot some notes on my laptop. The whole plan of writing in the motel isn't working because of the television and beer, and then in the morning we sleep past checkout time and the cleaning lady bangs on our door, annoyed and confused, and the front desk clerk calls to tell us it's past checkout time, and are we planning to stay another night? So the Waffle House is my working spot for now.

Shack is on the phone getting directions to the Jack Daniel's plant in Tennessee. That's our mission for today: Lynchburg, Tennessee. Take the free tour. Sip some Jack. We have plenty of time because there's no show tonight.

"Let's find some local flavor, baby," Shack says on the way. "You know JD brings out the worst in me. Every time I've done something stupid it's been from too much Jack."

Lynchburg is in the middle of nowhere. A tiny two-or-three-street town in the hills of eastern Tennessee. Every bottle of Jack in the entire world gets made here, which is hard to believe considering there seem to be about a hundred people in the town. A bunch of Phishheads have the same idea. Half a dozen cars are plastered with Phish stickers along the quiet Main Street.

Big disappointment: Lynchburg is a dry town in a dry county. No liquor sold here. No bars. No free samples after the tour. The one exception to the rule is the small gift shop inside the plant where you can buy special forty-dollar gold-label Jack bottles.

"You can only get this variety right here," the lady behind the counter says. "Won't find it anywhere else. It's a collector's item."

"Is that right?" Shack says, picking up a bottle.

"Special item you got there," she says.

"I don't know." He turns to me. "Forty bucks for a bottle of booze?"

"Your call."

"It *is* a special variety," Shack says. "And the bottle is pretty cool, don't you think?"

On the walking tour, we end up in a group with a couple of tie-dyed Phishheads. "Hey," one of them says, spotting Shack's bottle. "You could sell that at the show, man. Make some good money, no doubt. 'Special Jack! I got your shots of Special Jack! Two bucks!' "

"I'm keeping this." Shack curls the bottle in his arm. "I'm taking it home."

I want to ask them a whole bunch of questions for the book, but the tour guide keeps jabbering away and I don't get a chance. Plus, everyone huddles as close to the guide as possible because he's impossible to understand, standing there in his Wranglers and kick-ass boots, thumbs hooked on his belt buckle, explaining that these here charcoals are a very special charcoal that Mr. Daniel hisself chose for certain properties . . . Except this is only what I think he's saying. His mountain accent is fierce. What I really hear is: garbly garbly garbly Tennessee whiskey garbly garbly garbly Mr. Daniel hisself . . .

About six o'clock, after an early dinner of shredded beef and cole slaw in the Lynchburg church rec room (part of the weekend's Fourth of July celebration), we end up on a bench on the town green. Shack still clutches his bottle, taking it with him everywhere because he doesn't want it poisoned from sitting in the heat of the Jimmy. It's still about ninety-five degrees.

"I can't believe I spent forty bucks on a bottle of booze," Shack says.

"Let's get out of this town."

"I want to stay for the rodeo."

Supposedly in a couple of hours there will be a rodeo on the town green, though I don't see anything set up yet. Back at the church they were talking about it. This old guy in a blue hat, working the cash register, kept pointing at me and saying I'd be a good contestant for the rodeo. I ignored him and forked my shredded beef. But he kept it up, and Shack of course thought it was a great idea. At one point the man tipped his cap in some sort of gesture to me. I never said a word to the guy about the rodeo, expressed no interest in it whatsoever while he and Shack were talking at the end of the cafeteria line.

"I'm sick of this place," I say. "Let's get in the Jimmy and drive the hell out of here."

"We should stay, dude. I've never seen anything like it."

"It's depressing."

Three guys dressed for the rodeo saunter across the street. They look much too young to be in any kind of rodeo. Maybe sixteen years old, tops. And they're small, too. Three little skinny guys in tight jeans with gigantic cowboy hats. Actually, one of them wears shorts, which seems ridiculous with the extra-large belt buckle.

"Don't you want to see one of those boys get tossed?" Shack says. "There's a goddamn rodeo tonight. Can you believe this?"

"Not really. I don't feel like waiting around. This place is sapping all my energy. I've got nothing left. And this goddamn sun, I can't take it."

"This is America, man. We're in bumfuck Tennessee on the Fourth of July weekend. This is some local color!"

"I think it sucks."

"Look around. Where else are you going to find something like this? I love it. You're not into it, are you? I can tell you want to get out of here. But just look around."

"I'm *looking* around. I think it's boring."

"All right," Shack says. "Let's go."

"No. Fuck it. You're gonna be mad if we go."

"No I won't."

"Yeah you will. You already are."

"I don't want to stay if you're going to be miserable," Shack says.

"I just think we should press on to Atlanta. We'll get there a night early and we'll be in good shape for tomorrow night's show."

"Will you go out in Atlanta when we get there tonight?"

"Sure I will."

"You're not going to wimp out and say, 'Let's just stay in, it's kinda late'?"

"No. I'll go out. Definitely. I promise."

Back on the road, Shack has a decision to make. You see . . . well . . . he has this problem on the road with going to the bathroom . . . He can urinate, but that's it. I mention it here because it's become a fairly big part of the trip. He brings it up again and again and then doesn't want to talk about it. "I'm just not in a rhythm," he says. "I need a rhythm. I need to have a routine. But I don't want to talk about it. That makes it worse, talking about it." The decision he has tonight: whether or not to drink this bottle of greenish-yellowish fluid he bought at the drugstore. At the last pit stop he found a pharmacist in a quiet corner and asked a few hushed questions. He came out of the place with a bottle in a brown paper bag. For the last hour or so, the bottle has been rattling around the glove compartment.

"I can't decide whether to take it or not," Shack says. "What do you think?"

"Well, I don't know. What does it do?"

"It's strong stuff."

"How strong?"

"It flushes you out completely. Kicks in in about six hours."

"I guess take a teaspoon or whatever."

"No, you drink the whole bottle."

"Damn."

"All right, I'm just going to do it."

Atlanta, midnight. Perched on a bar patio overlooking a section of the city called Buckhead. Shack starts us off with a double shot of Jack Daniel's.

"No thanks," I say.

"Just drink it."

On line for more drinks. Vodka-and-tonics.

"This one's on me," I say.

"Dude, you're going to run out of money."

"You're right. I'm blowing my whole advance for the book. I can't believe how much this trip is costing."

"You better write a good book."

"Yeah, well—"

"Actually, fuck it. Even if you write a shitty book it'll still be a good time."

Shack has this thing he likes to do at a crowded bar. It's called taking a lap. He drains his glass, plunks it down on the counter, and walks slowly around the bar, scoping out the scene with a cigarette between his fingers. He looks for any group of girls that are (a) fairly attractive and (b) without guys. On the first lap, glancing casually about, he never makes a move. He comes back, orders another drink, smokes his cigarette, and chats quietly about the various prospects: "Table of blondes at two o'clock, but don't look now," or "The other side of the bar seems to have some more talent—let's finish these and head over."

Tonight, for whatever reason, he's really got it going. After lap number two he stops by a booth of laughing girls, all smoking, and asks for a light. A few seconds later, he slides into the booth. A few minutes later, he waves me over. A few hours later, we end up in the backseat of a car crowded with U Georgia sorority girls, tearing through a deserted six-lane highway at five a.m., heading back to some condo on the outskirts of Atlanta for more beer. Shack is *working* it. He has his shwerve on, which really is an incredible thing to see. It's like he was designed for this situation.

He's talking and talking and everyone's laughing. One girl in particular seems to be transfixed by Shack, sitting close beside him in the backseat. But he's more interested in a girl in the front seat, so he kind of leans forward and talks to the crew up front and every once in a while turns back to check on his Sure Thing. Everything he says is just cool and charming and funny. But then for a few seconds everything goes terribly wrong. Shack's carrying on and on, shouting about this and that, the highway roaring by in the dark, and for some reason—you're not going to believe this—he all of a sudden shouts, I mean *shouts*, at the top of his lungs, "VAGINA!"

(Now, I have no idea why he said it, neither does Shack, and I'm sort of embarrassed to mention it, especially looking at it now on my screen. But it was just this unbelievably strange moment, one of those moments where as it's happening you just know you'll remember it forever.)

His outburst is even weirder because it has absolutely nothing to do with whatever he's talking about, not part of any story. It's like he's on such a roll, doing so well, feeling so great, that he just sort of explodes. The look on his face is one of pure wild joy. In the minute of silence that follows, he looks horrified. He turns to me, mouth still open, eyes terrified. *What have I done? I've ruined everything....* He just keeps looking at me, afraid to look at anyone else in the car. Nobody speaks. At some point a female voice from up front says, "Well, well...."

But it doesn't ruin Shack's night with the woman sitting beside him. I think she becomes *more* fascinated. We all end up back at her place, a messy condo that reeks of cat. The two of them head for the bedroom and the rest of us head to the deck to escape the smell of cat. We sit on patio furniture, three of us, talking about all sorts of things, and after a while Shack cracks open the sliding glass door and asks to speak with me inside for a sec. His hair is messy.

"What do you want me to do?" Shack whispers, looking back at the bedroom door.

"I'll be fine."

"You sure?"

"Yeah. I'll just call a cab. Don't worry about me."

"I don't want to leave you hanging."

"I'm fine."

He heads back into the bedroom, where the cat smell seems to be most pungent.

I take a cab back to the Best Western. I find out the next day an interesting detail about what happened to Shack in the cat room: things were going great, moving along nicely, and then the green potion kicked in.

The Family Berzerker

July 3, Atlanta, Georgia

Terrible morning. Extremely hung over and sick. Barely functional. Jack Daniel's to blame.

Shack rolls into the Best Western about eleven a.m., back from his big night. I'm lying in bed with my laptop and scattered scraps of notes on the covers, not getting a thing done. Wimbledon on television in the background.

"I can't write this book," I say.

"Sure you can, dude. Who's winning?" Shack sits down on the edge of the bed and turns up the volume.

"No. It's not working. We go out every night and in the morning I can't remember a goddamn thing."

"What about all those times last night when I was like, 'Listen, you gotta remember this for the book'? Remember that?"

"Yeah, I remember you saying that, but about what? What was I supposed to remember?"

"Wait a minute. Wasn't it . . . you know, yeah . . . wasn't . . . it? Shit, never mind. No clue. I can't remember."

"And look at me. I can't write. I can't even get out of bed. I'm shaking for chrissake."

"Listen, we'll sit down and talk about it later. You know, will have a little sesh, me and you, and you can type it right into the computer. When's the Sampras match?"

Now it's three-thirty p.m., a couple hours before the first Atlanta show, and I'm back at the Waffle House. There must

be a million Waffle Houses in the South. You see them more
often than McDonald's. Across the street is the Motel 6, our new
headquarters for the next two days, where right now Shack is
taking his afternoon nap with the curtains drawn and the air conditioner cranked. Before he dozed off he said, "You gotta focus,
dude. You have a book to write. Get up and go to the Waffle
House." I told him to shut up and that he doesn't have to remind
me. But he's right. So here I am. The good thing about this place
is you can stay for hours and no one asks any questions. Like my
waitress seems to be fine with me just ordering a grilled cheese,
eating a few bites, and sitting here taking up a whole booth for
two hours. I don't think I'm going to make it to the end of the
tour. It's only July 3. Three days into the journey and I'm struggling to hold on. I'm not drinking a drop of alcohol tonight.

And it's time to do some damn interviews. I mean, I need to
talk with people, gather information. So I head out to the motel's
pool with the mini tape recorder in my pocket. A few Phishheads
are floating in the water. One woman with long brown hair sits
on the edge with her legs dangling in.

"Hi," she says with a southern accent.

"Hi."

"Come on in. It's nice."

"Well, actually . . ." I'm like this close to taking out my tape
recorder and giving my whole schpiel. "The thing is, I'm writing
a book about the tour, and would you mind if I turn on this tape
machine and ask you a few questions?" But I don't do it. I chicken
out. It feels weird—like what's-her-name who studied the goril-
las in Africa, sitting on a stump and watching them. Phishheads
are strange people. And they know it. Which makes writing
about them, or at least interviewing them, a bit tricky. I don't
want to be Mr. Reporter with the tape machine. It's kind of
pathetic, I know, since there's a book to write. Instead of clicking
on the Record button and firing away, I say, "Yeah, a swim
sounds good. Water's nice? I'll have to go and change."

So I go back to the room, ditch my tape recorder, and change into my bathing suit for a swim. I figure I'll just tell them about the book after I dive in.

"We've sold everything on tour," the woman dangling her legs says. "Grilled cheese, beer, water." Her name is Heather and she's from South Carolina, twenty-five years old, and has been doing the tour for years. She's pretty, in a waify, limby kind of way. Looks a bit undernourished. "We've even sold banana pancakes," Heather says. "After doing nitrous all night or whatever, people aren't going to want to take out the grill for like one pancake. So we have them ready. Banana pancakes and Bloody Marys."

I swim around asking questions, and when I can't think of a new one to ask I hold my breath, drop to the bottom, and think of something else to say.

"I'm out of cash already," Heather says. "I quit like three jobs to come on tour. I was working at this sewing place. My mom was like, '*Why* are you going? What are you doing? You're in so much debt.' I told her the debt will be there when I get back, you know, it's not going anywhere. And like why not? Why not go? I don't have kids. I don't have a husband."

I ask her why she goes on tour. She says for the music, and then I say what about the friends and the adventure and all that? She thinks about that for a second and says that yeah the friends are a big part of it, too, definitely, and the adventure.

Then she wants to know: "Are you just writing the book for yourself and then trying to sell it after?"

"No, I have a contract."

This question doesn't surprise me. You meet a lot of "artists" on tour. Poets, philosophers, painters. But their work is rarely in evidence—e.g., painters without brushes, poets with Magic Marker pens and flowery notebooks filled with nothing but Phish set lists.

Heather is on tour with her friend, also named Heather, who plans to get a Ph.D. in anthropology, I think she said. She wants to write about Phishheads in the future, maybe for a thesis. Her boyfriend, hanging back in the parking lot, working on their van,

walks over a couple of times but doesn't say anything. He's apparently in the planning stages to write a guide book called *The Hippie Atlas*, with directions to concert venues, shortcuts, fast routes, that sort of thing.

"Did you go to Nashville?" Heather Number Two says from her lounge chair.

"We did but, ah, we didn't make it to the show. The storm slowed us down and we didn't make it on time."

"You missed it? It was the best I've seen in years. The boys were on! They were tight. Ronnie McCoury and Tim O'Brien sat in."

"Who's that?" I say, swimming sidestroke.

"What?" Heather Number Two says.

"Tim O'Brien, who's that?"

"You don't know those guys? They're legends in bluegrass. Total legends. And you could tell the boys were so psyched to have them up on stage. They're like heroes for them. It's the best I've heard them play in years."

The interviews are going pretty well at this point, I'm thinking. Then Shack comes out to the pool, groggy-eyed from his nap, crashes into the water with the Nerf football, and the interview ends. We chuck the football around the pool while some wild ten-year-old kid climbs on our backs, swiping for the ball, not responding to Shack's repeated question, "Where are your parents?"

I walk back to my room in a wet bathing suit and glance sideways into the room next to ours. The scene hasn't changed all day. Through a partially curtained window: seven or eight guys sprawled on the bed, smoking pot and watching television, the air conditioner blasting away. Probably watching the Motel 6's free HBO. It's about three o'clock. Soon this group will shower, probably eat lunch/dinner at the Waffle House across the street, and head out to the preshow parking-lot festivities, really get the night started.

In an attempt to have a mellow night, I've sworn off the parking-lot scene. Shack seems okay with this, sort of.

We get to the show at seven-thirty p.m. and find our seats a few minutes before the lights go down. On my left is a middle-aged couple from Key West. She looks hippieish and wrinkly from the sun and kind of out-to-lunch. He's tall and long-haired, in a tank top, and also looks out-to-lunch. She rolls a joint slowly and seems bored. On their way north, she says, to a big fair where they plan to set up shop for a week. She tells me what they plan to sell at the fair, but she goes into this whole thing and halfway through I have no idea what she's talking about. I think they're both pretty high already. She's had enough of Key West, she says. "I'm kinda getting sick of it. I've been there twenty-five years. Too long."

You don't see too many of these graying sixties types on tour. They definitely stand out. There's something sad about the sight of a tie-dyed, potbellied fifty-something at a Phish show. Like life has passed them by. You never felt this way at Dead shows in the mid-nineties because there were so many middle-aged hippies dancing in the aisles. It was *their* scene after all—their band, their music, their generation, their spirit. But now it's thirty years after the summer of '69, thirty years after this dazed and worn-out Key West couple was young and on the move, with everything in front of them. And here they are at a Phish show, rolling their millionth joint, not quite familiar with the music, no friends to hang out with between sets, nothing to say really. Old and tired and quiet, rolling downhill towards sixty surrounded by all these young people.

To my right, next to Shack, a teenage couple can't keep their hands off each other. It's getting embarrassing. Groping and kissing and smiling. Shack keeps tapping my knee while I'm talking to the Key West lady, jerking his head in the young couple's direction.

"I know," I say. "I see. I see."

"This is ridiculous," he says. "Look at them."

They really are quite shameless. She wears bell-bottoms and a tight shirt and sways her hips. More like grinds. He has a hat on backwards and long shorts and keeps his hands on her hips and his body pressed tight. I bet they're on Ecstasy. You see this sort of thing fairly often among the cleaner-cut-looking couples— over-the-top displays of affection, especially when the lights go down. My guess is that these two are from around here. Maybe seventeen or eighteen years old, from the Atlanta suburbs. This is their only Phish show of the summer. Or maybe they're coming tomorrow night, too. But they're definitely not on tour for the long haul. They don't have the look: weary, dirty, scruffy. Plus, she has shaved armpits. Sorry, but it's a dead giveaway. You don't see women with shaved pits on tour very often. It's pretty much standard fare to go au naturel. You also don't ever see the hardcore Phishheads—the dreadlocked doin'-the-whole-tour crew—in this type of blatantly sexual embrace. They hug each other all the time, sure. In fact, they hug everyone. I've never seen so much hugging. But never anything approaching sex. Not even a long kiss. Phishheads, men and women, seem to to be

oddly sexless. They walk around with very little clothing, sometimes even naked, but there's nothing sexy about most of them.
The not-showering and the tangled hair and the ugly clothes certainly don't help. But it's more in the facial expressions—kind of
a mix between uninterested and spacey.

A quick theory: life on tour—sleeping in buggy tents, riding in
sweaty cars, using disgusting Porta Potties—diminishes substan-
tially one's sex drive.

Phish starts off the night with a tune called "Chalkdust Torture"—a classic, and one of my favorites. The whole song
builds up to these lines, well-known in Phish circles:

> Can't this wait till I'm old?
> Can't I live while I'm young?
> Can't I live while I'm young?
> Can't I live while I'm young?

Like most Phish songs, "Chalkdust Torture" doesn't make
much sense. It begins with the lyric:

> Come stumble my mirth beaten worker
> I'm Jesmond the Family Berzerker

I've heard this song, I don't know, a hundred times and have
no idea what it's about. Something about this guy Jesmond and a
flagon of rice and then he goes around and, well, I really don't
know what happens. But I love the song, and I love that line—
"Can't this wait till I'm old?"—because I think it's funny and
because I think it kind of sums up the attitude of fans on tour,
escaping the normal routines of a grown-up life. Can't I live
while I'm young? Can't I hit the road and lead a rootless life and
have no responsibilities? Come on, at least for a while?

It doesn't matter really what the songs are about. Phish

doesn't sing about the times they are a-changin', or falling in and out of love. They sing about Jesmond the Family Berzerker and his strange adventures. With Phish it's almost a different language. A quick sample of lyrics from a few songs:

Won't you step into the freezer
Uncle Ebenezer

Guyute was the ugly pig
who walked on me and danced a jig . . .
he lectured me in language strange
and scampered quickly out of range

Give the director
a serpent deflector
a mud rat detector
a ribbon reflector

These are not lyrics I picked flipping through a Phish songbook, looking for the weirdest or strangest. These are typical, just lyrics off the top of my head from three songs that come to mind. In fact, there is a book called *The Phishing Manual* that tries to explain some of the songs, but even the manual itself, in trying to explain these oddball lyrics, comes across as pretty oddball itself.

Sam Ankerson, the Strangefolk guy, said, "I've always paralleled them to *Seinfeld*. They sort of rose at the same time. *Seinfeld*'s whole credo was like, 'We have a very strict rule around here: it's just comedy for the sake of comedy, nothing else.' That's why you never saw an episode of *Seinfeld* get serious, the way *Cheers* got serious, the way *M*A*S*H* got serious, the way *All in the Family* got serious. Just strictly comedy, never taking yourself too seriously. I think Phish maybe was the same way, especially when the Grateful Dead was still around. They were so desperate to not be lumped into the Grateful Dead. It was basically: 'We are incredibly precise, but fun music for the sake of fun, rock and roll for the sake of rocking.' It was only after the Grateful Dead went away that who knows why but they seemed to be like: 'We're songwriters now.' And they've started to write lyrics now and I don't think they've pulled it off."

It's weird, if you think about it, that the band in the U.S. with the strongest, most devoted following sings songs about nothing really, songs without any kind of meaning or message. But it also makes perfect sense. Rock and roll is not about getting across a message. It was at some point, I guess. In the sixties. But I say that only because I've read it and of course everyone sort of thinks that. I listen to Bob Dylan today because I like the style of his lyrics, the mood he evokes, the music itself, the way he writes about heartbreak. And he can turn a phrase like no other songwriter. There's no message in the Rolling Stones, and they truly are the best rock and roll band in the world. For the Stones, it's about ripping through a song with a strong guitar and some nasty lyrics.

I'm wandering here. It doesn't matter that Phish's lyrics aren't about anything concrete or important or counterculturish—you can still be moved by songs about the Guelah Papyrus and the Wolfman's Brother because it's the music itself that moves you or makes you dance or shout, not the meaning of the lyrics.

For the encore, Fishman comes out by himself with a snare drum under his arm. Under the spotlight he sings "The Little Drummer Boy," making the lyrics up as he goes along . . . *Pa rum pa pum pum, ra pa pum pum* . . . Everyone loves Fishman because he's a complete nut. There he is in front of thirty thousand people standing in a dress with a pair of goggles strapped to his head singing "The Little Drummer Boy." (His other favorite thing to do: occasionally he hauls out a vacuum cleaner, which he keeps stashed under his drum set, carries it to the front of the stage and blows a tune into the nose piece of the whirring machine. It comes out sounding like one of those awful plastic kazoo party favors you get at New Year's parties.)

NUBAR ALEXANIAN

We head backstage to the aftershow party. We have two stickers on our t-shirts that get us through security. They say PHISH AFTERSHOW with a picture of Kojak—the detective—in a derby. (No idea.) The stickers are cool, and people in the general crowd definitely look twice when they see them. "Aftershow . . . Dude, you got any more of those?" The aftershow isn't that exciting. It doesn't really take place backstage, more like in a VIP tent. And it's not very VIP. Just a bunch of ordinary people standing around drinking beer and eating chips and glancing over their shoulders, hoping the band will show up. Which they never do. Actually, Mike Gordon, the bassist, comes out for a while. I've been to a bunch of these aftershows and Gordon usually makes the rounds. He's a small guy with truly gigantic hair. Sometimes Fishman turns up at the aftershow, charges around a bit in his black sneakers. He's even smaller than Mike. Like a little bearded kid. Trey and Page never show up because, well, probably they would get swamped and they'd rather not.

I suppose I should go talk to Mike. Maybe get a quote. Maybe get a closer look at that hair. But he's talking to someone. And no one else seems to be making a move in his direction, though I'm sure the entire aftershow crew is collectively aware of his every step. I talk about whatever with Shack, and like everyone else keep one eye on the door to see who comes through next. One thing to note: just about every woman back here is attractive.

Every armpit hairless. No Hardcores at the VIP. Much more put-together crowd, no hippie clothes or dreadlocks in sight. Do you know what Def Leppard used to do? They had someone go out into the audience during a concert and round up the best-looking women for the postshow festivities. (I saw it on VH1's *Behind the Music* series.)

Outside the aftershow a bunch of fans linger in the dark, craning their necks to see past security, maybe get a glimpse of the band. One of them looks at me and my sticker with a kind of awe, then he peers back into the tent. I think he might make a run for it when the security guy turns his head.

I recently met a woman in her fifties (off the tour) and we got to talking about my book. I was explaining to her the project when she said, "Oh, yes, I've heard of that. It's sort of like stalking." She's right. There is a stalking element to this whole fan thing . . . following these four guys everywhere, trying to find out which hotel they're staying in, spreading stories about who was spotted where, setting up Web sites devoted to the band. I'd say this guy peering into the tent, desperate to get inside, perhaps ready to run for it, qualifies as stalker material.

Atlanta General

July 5, Folly Beach, South Carolina. Past midnight.

Much-needed rest from the tour. Here now for two days at a beach house on the water. Not quite possible for me to write an entry for last night, the Fourth of July, for reasons which will soon become clear. So Shack and I took the tape recorder out tonight, sat down on the front porch, and talked through the last twenty-four hours, starting with yesterday afternoon in the parking lot before the Atlanta holiday show, right before we gobbled up some "extra-dank" brownies. Here is some of the conversation:

ME: I guess I'd like to start. I'd like to know—when we were leaning against the car there and the two brownie people came up to us, they were perfectly normal looking, right?

SHACK: Yeah, for a Phish show, dude, they were pretty well put together. They had their brownies separately wrapped, and they said, "Would you like to buy some brownies?"

ME: But the thing is, looking back on it now, they never said *pot* brownies.

SHACK: They said brownies.

ME: And you said, "What do you got in them?" or something like that.

SHACK: Did I?

ME: Yeah, somehow it came up that they said, "Do you want the dank or the extra-dank?"

SHACK: Right. Well, they were just giving us our options. And since I wanted a hard buzz—although that was right after I went from like a two to a five.* Remember, I had a thirty-second span when I got hammered.

ME: Yeah, you already had a bunch of beers at that point. So we bought the brownies for like—

SHACK: They said, "Extra-dank, two for six bucks." It was fucking cheap.

ME: Right. Two extra-dank for six bucks.

SHACK: You ate yours right away.

ME: Immediately.

SHACK: You needed a buzz.

ME: I needed a buzz.

SHACK: It was right after my little pep talk about "engaging."†

ME: Yup. Exactly. I was ready to go.

SHACK: Now, did you feel pressure to do it?

ME: No. None. I was happy. I didn't even feel nervous about eating the brownie because I figured it was, you know, a marijuana brownie, not a big deal. Make me feel a little light-headed, that's it.

SHACK: So you took the brownie like on the spot?

ME: Yeah. Probably around six-thirty, I would guess.

SHACK: And I wanted to save mine 'cause I knew I was going to hit a low and I wanted to eat it when I was going to hit a low during the show.

ME: So we walk around and have another beer or two.

SHACK: Yup.

ME: We end up back at the car—

SHACK: And you're still not feeling it?

ME: No, I'm feeling fine. You asked me at one point, you're like, "How are you doing?" I said, "Fine. It's not a big deal." And then right when we were at the car, before we were about to

---

*Rating system for your beer buzz, based on a one-to-ten scale.
†More like a fifteen-minute speech about how if I want to write this book I have to show some balls and go up and talk to people, get involved . . . i.e., "You can't just stand here leaning against the car all day."

walk to the stadium, I started to feel it creep up. And all I can describe is that I felt it first in my eyeballs. It felt very tingly. And then beyond that it felt like a really good rush—I mean, it felt like—

SHACK: So you had a good buzz going?

ME: Yeah, I had a good buzz going. But it wasn't too much. It was fun. It was, ah, it was really intense.

SHACK: Like why? Were you noticing stuff?

ME: I felt very floaty.

SHACK: Floaty?

ME: Right.

SHACK: So you weren't like being a super-hyper observer of what was going on?

ME: No, no. It wasn't hallucinogenic at all. I mean, it was just very floaty. It was like the perfect, you know, two-beer buzz taken to the next degree, know what I mean? Very doable.

SHACK: Two quick beers.

ME: Two quick beers to your head. That's what it felt like. So then we're walking to the stadium and I'm starting to freak out a little bit. I'm like, "Shack, you gotta eat your brownie, you gotta, you gotta eat your brownie." And you kept saying no, but you caved in at some point—you caved in roughly an hour after I ate mine.

SHACK: Right.

ME: We show up at the front gate, ticket in hand—

SHACK: So we get to the gate and we have our tickets and the night before we got in the VIP entrance and this time the guy negged us at the VIP entrance, which you were fine, ticket in hand, ready to go in.

ME: Now you think this is the turning point for me?

SHACK: I think that what happened in the next two minutes is totally the turning point because we got negged there, we turned around to where we had to go, which was like in the middle of—there's only one entrance to this place, right, and every fucking person had to go through this entrance. The hugest fucking crowd.

And I think you took one look at that and said, "There's no fucking way that I can do that."

ME: Right. That's exactly what I said.

SHACK: And then that's when you sat down and said, "I need a minute." And I tried to parlay that you were fucked up a little bit into getting back into the VIP entrance because you couldn't deal with the crowd.*

ME: At what point did the medic show up?

SHACK: You asked for one.

ME: Right.

SHACK: Then they showed up and I don't remember what they asked you.

ME: I just know this big muscular guy who might as well have been a bouncer—he had like biker shorts and a tight white t-shirt and all these things clipped to him, like pagers clipped to him. And he grabbed me by the elbow and sort of carted me off.

SHACK: He didn't ask you any questions there or anything?

ME: No, he asked me what I had had and I told him I had a brownie and he gave me the oh-you've-had-a-*brownie* look.

SHACK: Was that the first extra-dank question you threw out?

ME: Probably that was the first one.

SHACK: I just need to add that you solicited the opinion of everybody about what "extra-dank" meant.

ME: And I never got an answer. I still need to find that out. So then—

SHACK: I think there's more that happened here. No conversation or anything?

ME: Not that I can remember. I just know that he grabbed my elbow and next thing I know he's walking me past that huge crowd, which made me scared just to look at it, and took me to

---

*Shack did indeed try to "parlay" my problem to our advantage by walking back to the VIP gate, talking with security while pointing back at me (slumped on the ground), making a case along the lines of, "You don't want me to take *him* through the main gate with all those people, do you?"

the infirmary, at which point I'm freaking out. It's like I want my life to end, that's how bad it is.

SHACK: Okay, but wait. You got to go through this. What did they ask? What were you doing?

ME: I remember one obnoxious EMT type, this lady with dreadlocks—after I was lying down quivering she was like, "*Why did you eat the brownie?*" and I said, "Well, I thought it was going to give me a nice buzz. I didn't think it was going to send me over the edge."

SHACK: Were people paying attention to you while you were lying down?

ME: Not really.

SHACK: Describe the room.

ME: It looked like an RV trailer with wood paneling around and fluorescent lighting above, and every once in a while someone's beeper would go off, which would scare the piss out of me. There was a woman across from me who was huddled in some kind of shawl, shaking. There was a guy directly across from me very upset about something. I'm not sure what. Ah . . . there was just a general feeling of . . . of . . . I've just never been so terrified, absolutely terrified. I couldn't think about anything else except the terror. It's like, imagine you're walking along and there's a stalker behind a tree and you don't know anything about it and all of a sudden the stalker comes at you and you see the ax blade in the night—that one second of realization even before the fight begins, that one second, imagine that consistently for three hours.

SHACK: That's how it felt?

ME: Yup.

SHACK: Do you remember anything specific that crossed your mind?

ME: I'm not sure really. Just fear. At some point I thought, There's no fucking way I'm writing this book. I'm done with it. I hate this scene. That's it, you know. Done with the whole thing. Going home . . . And wait, where were *you*? . . . You were coming in and out of the trailer at this point.

SHACK: I got kicked out.

ME: You got kicked out for stealing candy, right?

SHACK: They had like these bins and I thought it was for people waiting for their friends. They had like Snickers and Tootsie
Rolls and Tootsie Pops, and so I opened up the bin and the lady
screamed at me and told me to get out and wait outside.

ME: Did you have your hat on at that point?*

SHACK: I think I took it off because of the trailer. So I'm outside
with people that weren't sick enough to go inside. I got one dude
that had a bloody chin, one guy that was so high—high and
hot—that he passed out and was drinking water. It was kind of a
chaotic scene. That's when I talked to this fat Phish fan about
what stuff gets laced in the brownies. She basically said that they
rarely lace brownies with acid. They lace it with other shit. She
said it was probably just a really strong ganja brownie. I was like,
"Are you sure?" and she was like, "Yeah, that's what I think." So
that's when I got my first notion that it wasn't really such a big
deal.† I went back in the trailer twice. The second time that little
kid was complaining when they said call his parents, and I was
like, "Listen, dude, there's nothing you can say that's going to get
you out of this, so shut up."

ME: And they got mad at you, right?

SHACK: Yeah, that's when they told me to sit outside again.

ME: What did I look like? Was I sweating or howling or crying
or anything?

SHACK: No, no. You were lying there moving your legs. And
like anyone that was nearby, anyone, you'd be like, "Do you
know what 'extra-dank' means?" You were very inquisitive, you
know what I mean. And that was the first time you asked me if
you could just get knocked out.

---

*Shack had a giant red-white-and-blue hat that stood about two feet high and
made him look like a Dr. Seuss character and didn't help my general anxiety level.
†Basically, Shack thought I was being a big cry baby who couldn't deal with a bit
of a buzz. Soon enough he would find out for himself . . .

ME: Right. And that became the steady question the rest of the night.

SHACK: And no one gave you the answer you wanted.

ME: And the reason why I went to the hospital from there is because I requested it?

SHACK: Exactly. You said, "I want to go to the hospital," and I was like, Fuck . . .

ME: And at this point you're not feeling much of anything?

SHACK: I'm buzzing. I'm buzzing hard. But I'm feeling like totally rational. And that's part of the reason why I was mad— the show has just started, I'm not buzzing that hard and this guy is fucking flipping out. The first time I knew something was up though was outside the trailer when I was talking to these three dudes who I thought for sure were brothers. They looked exactly the same. I said, "Hey, you guys are brothers." And they said, "No we're not." And then I was like, "Oh, okay, then just the two of you, then, huh?" "No we're not brothers, man." I thought they were triplets.

ME: So then I'm in the ambulance.

SHACK: And there was a second guy in the ambulance with you.

ME: Oh . . . yeah . . . yeah. . . . He just kept saying, "I want to go home, I want to go home, I want to go home." I just wanted that guy out of the ambulance. He was causing me so much stress. I wanted him out of there.

SHACK: Well, the thing is, he wanted to go home but he had asked to go to the hospital, which is the only reason he was in the ambulance in the first place. And then they let him just walk out into the parking lot. He walked out of the ambulance. He went from going to the hospital to going to his car and smoking up again.

ME: So in the hospital is when I get the IV in my arm?

SHACK: No, dude, in the ambulance.

ME: So I'm in the ambulance—

SHACK: They take your vitals, they relay it to Atlanta General or whatever the hospital is, and then he gives you the Narcan.

And the guy up front is telling me it could be anything from nothing to PCP. That's the range.

ME: Did you ask him what would happen if it was PCP?

SHACK: Yeah, I think I might've. I think he just said, you know, "Give him some shit and let him ride if off." Then he started telling me about this guy who almost drowned in the lake the night before, a Phishhead. He was telling me about all these different things he saw and was just fat and indifferent. I would say those are the two best words to describe him.

ME: So then we get to the hospital.

SHACK: And I had to stay behind and talk to the check-in lady and fill out your paperwork. So I wasn't with you for about twenty-five minutes. I don't know what happened to you when you were in there. I was answering questions about you.

ME: What kind of questions were they asking? Basics?

SHACK: Yeah. They needed factual information.

ME: And then . . . okay, so fast-forward for a sec—

SHACK: No, tell me what happened when you went in.

ME: Well, I don't remember. I just remember freaking out and wanting to die.

SHACK: You don't remember if someone came and saw you right away or were you left alone?

ME: I didn't have the feeling that I was left alone. I had the feeling that there was activity in the room, there were people moving in and out, in and out. But none of it mattered. Whether someone was mopping my forehead or whether someone was walking outside the room, there was this feeling of terror that wouldn't have subsided if someone was sitting on my lap.

SHACK: You don't remember any of the details of any of the conversations when you first went in?

ME: No. Not one. Not a one. So, wait, what happened to you?

SHACK: It wasn't until about twenty minutes into your hospital stay that I really got throttled. I was fucking really amped up. I got scared when I couldn't find the bathroom. I got lost. I had really bad cotton mouth. I couldn't breathe. I got lost. I kept walking past this security guard pretending to know where I was going. He was watching me and I thought I was going to get arrested. I've never been so scared in my life. It's hard to describe. Like I didn't know where to go with all these doors. Everything looked the same. You go through the wrong door and you're further away from where you want to go. So I was fucking petrified. If I can piece it back together as best as I can, I talked to the doctor a few times, listened in on some conversations, came back in, was completely mesmerized by electronic equipment. I'm watching your heartbeat, I'm watching your respiration. And like anytime it would go under ten I would go over and wake you up.

ME: Wake me up, that's right. You'd tap me and I'd open my eyes and you were standing there going, "Say something! Say something!" which didn't help out my situation at all.

SHACK: It looked low. I don't know the freakin' numbers. But it looked low. So I wanted you to talk. Basically, it was you were falling asleep and relaxing but I wasn't making the connection.

ME: Right.

SHACK: And then I ran into this other Phish dude who was talking my head off, so happy to find me but making zero sense. Then I talked to the doctor and he said you were fine, just really scared. "We gave him this, we gave him that," he said, "but he's totally stable and whenever he's ready, he goes." And that's when I went back in and sat back down and observed the whole catheter thing.* And finally I got so wigged out, I wanted to go so bad that I started to talk to you.

ME: That's when I woke up.

SHACK: That's when you woke up. And kinda started laughing.

ME: Right. I realized with so much relief that my mind was back. Still not there, but at least back to earth. And I saw that you were wired and thought that you needed to be hooked up.

---

*In the bed next to mine, separated by a curtain, a very large older woman was getting a catheter. The nurses couldn't get it properly stuck in there and Shack couldn't help watching the whole thing. I think it finally put him over the edge.

SHACK: Yeah, you were trying to convince me to switch places with you and I knew that I couldn't do that. I couldn't handle that. And then you got better and better and then within like ten minutes you were taking care of me.

From here I can piece together the last moments of the night. I woke up in the hospital bed around midnight. When I came to, I saw Shack at the end of the bed with his hands covering his face, peering sideways at the catheter saga next door. I heard some sheets rustling behind the curtain but I couldn't see anything. Shack saw everything and he was very upset. Someone unhooked me from the machine and we left the room very slowly. When we got to the phone to call a cab, Shack panicked.

"I can't do it," he said. "I can't make the phone call. I can't dial the numbers."

I took the phone out of his hand and called the cab.

A long ride back to the Motel 6, the whole time Shack carrying on, "I need to hang out! You gotta hang out with me! I can't go to sleep yet!" He was yelling at me.

"Fine," I said. "We'll hang out."

We went straight to the Waffle House. I ordered a grilled cheese and didn't eat it. Shack smoked a lot of cigarettes. I couldn't stay for long.

"Dude, you gotta stay," Shack said. "Just hang out with me. I can't go back to the room yet. Hang out, will you?"

"I have to go back to the room. I can't stay here. It's too much."

"Look, we should stay together. Come on!"

He was pissed, but I had to go. I left him there sucking on his cigarette, peering around the place nervously. I walked back to the room and buried myself under the covers.

In the morning, the two Heathers gave us a ride in their van. We had to get the Jimmy, which was back at the parking lot. I sat in the front, not looking very good.

"I'm sorry you don't feel well," Heather Number One said. "You look like a different person than yesterday."

"Yeah. I sort of feel different."

"Here, write me your address and I'll send you a letter."

"Okay."

Our sleeping bags were strewn on the ground outside the Jimmy. Strange, I thought. Then I noticed the shattered window.

"We've been robbed!" Shack said.

I called 911 from a pay phone on the corner. Not a very nice neighborhood—I didn't even notice the broken-down homes and burnt-out cars last night because there were forty thousand Phishheads walking around.

The cop car arrived a few minutes later. From porches, front steps, windows, everyone in the neighborhood watched the cop car as it drove slowly down the street towards us.

"I can't believe you boys left your car here last night," the policewoman said. "This is a bad area. People around here could have had your whole car stripped in two minutes. You're lucky there's anything left. You're lucky you still have a car."

"I can't believe they took my forty-dollar bottle of Jack," Shack muttered.

Recovery

July 6, Folly Beach, South Carolina

Swimming in the ocean, regaining strength. Walking around barefoot and sleeping in sandy sheets. No show for two nights in a row feels like a long time.

Shack and I now have membership cards at the Sand Dollar Social Club—a dingy bar near the water with pool tables and dollar Bud cans. A year's membership costs a buck, and you get a pink Sand Dollar card with rules on the back which you have to sign, including: "The Sand Dollar Social Club may revoke membership at any time with or without legal cause." The bartender is pretty—blond hair in a ponytail, squarish little glasses, a long dress and sandals. A grad student paying the bills, is my guess. Shack spends two nights trying to make small talk with her, smoking cigarettes, glancing her way while chalking his pool stick. No luck.

Doing Who Knows What

July 7, Charlotte, North Carolina

I drop Shack off at the Charlotte International Airport, Delta terminal, and head over to American Airlines to pick up my friend Will, who's coming on tour for a while. On the way to the American terminal, a strange thing happens. I'm walking through the airport and start to feel kind of nervous. About nothing. Just nervous for no reason. And my legs all of a sudden feel twitchy. And then I think, *My God, the brownie's back.* Which doesn't help my nerves, just the thought of it. I head for the bathroom, duck into a stall, and bolt the door. But then that feels spooky. I leave quickly and head to my gate: B-12. Then it gets weird. I develop this unexplainable anxiety about gate B-12. Just the thought of gate B-12 increases the nervousness and twitching, and I think, *Oh no, not again, please no. . . .* A security guy motors by in a golf cart and I almost hop on and say, "Take me *out* of here." I keep walking, stopping at every water fountain because I think water will flush out the brownie remnants and because I'm stalling as I get closer to you-know-what gate.

When I spot B-12 I shiver. I cross the aisle and head for gate B-14, pick a seat away from other people and stare at the wall. Get a grip. You're fine. Nothing can happen to you here in B-14. . . . When Will's plane comes in, just walk across the aisle and wave from outside the gate.

(This probably sounds absurd, like my nerves have taken over and created something out of nothing. But I find out later—when I talk to Shack the next day on the phone—that he felt weird in the airport, too. "Yeah, when I woke up that day I felt sort of

strange—buzzing, kind of. All over. My whole body. I didn't
mention it, though, because it wasn't that strong. Just kind of
there. Then in the airport it came back. Not as bad as yours from
the sound of it.")

Will's plane lands an hour late. Which turns out to be a good
thing for me—time to ride this out. Will is a financial analyst in
San Francisco. He makes a lot of money and works a lot of hours.
This is a vacation for him and I don't want to cause a scene right
from the get-go.

Two minutes after his arrival I launch into the whole poison
brownie story. I told myself to wait and give him time, but I can't
help it. Will listens to the whole thing but isn't quite sure what to
make of it. Something about it doesn't make sense to him. He's
very practical-minded.

"So how does it feel?" he says. "Like right now what's going
on?"

"I don't know, really. Just nervous. Really nervous. And sort of
twitchy."

"Huh."

We get to the show late. I'm barely hanging on and a bit concerned about being in the crowd. Also concerned about the light
show. Phish has a pretty elaborate light display with spinning
shapes and strobes and all sort of colors. I don't want anything to
trigger the brownie juices. I'm also staying clear of the restroom,
which you wouldn't believe it in there—shoulder-to-shoulder
and hot thick air like a sauna and all sorts of muck on the floor.
Everyone talks in the bathroom. It's quite social. You talk to the
person standing beside you at the urinal or join into the general
conversation. And when you step up to your spot there's no pressure to keep your eyes glued to the wall. People look this way and
that, chatting all the while. During any thirty-second period at
the wall there are at least three or four conversations going on.

"Good first set, huh?"

"That's what I'm talking about—Trey was *on*, bro!"

"Hey, who's got an extra Virginia? I need one Virginia."

"I'm expecting something big next set, maybe 'Antelope,' you know. I think we're due."

"That dude down there at the end with the hat has an extra Virginia. Yo, my man here wants your Virginia."

"You need a Virginia? Hang on, I'll be right there. Actually, wait, hold on—meet me right outside like in a minute."

"Yo, stop fucking with the lights. I need to see in here."

"So you're riding with Larry, huh?"

"Picked me up in Atlanta, dude. He's got the van all fixed up, know what I'm saying? Put a couch in there and pillows, little carpet."

"Enough with the lights!"

"Yeah, 'Antelope' would be cool. I could go for a 'Hood' opener."

"Yo, Larry!"

It's not unusual for half the guys in the bathroom to go barefoot. They slop through as if walking on nice wet grass, totally unconcerned with what's squishing between their toes. They pad out of the bathroom leaving a trail of footmarks around the venue. Usually when the bathroom gets this crowded, guys find other spots to go—sometimes on the wall outside the restroom. But that's not the case here, what with a heavy security presence patrolling the grounds. Charlotte has a bad reputation among Phishheads, a place where you'll get busted for doing anything even slightly suspect. When Will went to find a bathroom in the bushes (despite my warnings), he heard some rustling in the next bush over. But he couldn't see anyone. "Hey!" a voice hissed from the bushes. "Get down! I'm back here, too." Normally, fans would not be concerned about this sort of thing. But the MO here in Charlotte seems to be: Don't push your luck. Before I left for the summer tour a Phish friend called up and said, "Be careful in Charlotte. I wouldn't do anything there. That place is bad news." Word travels quickly in this community. It's a safe bet that everyone on tour knows to lay low in Charlotte.

I'm also avoiding the lawn tonight. Every amphitheater on

tour has a lawn behind the pavilion which is general admission and can be a total disaster—muddy, steep, people passed out here and there. But sometimes it's not so bad, and each night between sets I leave my seat to find a small patch of open grass on the lawn. I lie down for a minute and look up at the sky. I take Will's cell phone out of my pocket, dial my home number, and talk to Jill. Our conversations aren't going so well. She asks me about the trip and I say it's fine and tell her about whatever we did today. We talk about her work. She's doing a rotation in urology this month and I hear some pretty gruesome cases while lying there on the lawn. As she talks about the day's operations, I picture her in blue scrubs and a blue mask, looking down at the patient on the table, hoping she'll maybe get to do a few stitches this time. She probably pictures me with a beer in one hand and a joint in the other. We're not connecting. You know that feeling when both of you know it and no one says anything? That's what it's like. It's a bad feeling. I wonder, though, how could it be different? I knew when I hit the road on this rock and roll journey she wouldn't like it—up all hours, doing who knows what. I wonder how the guys in the band deal with this with their wives. Three of them are married. What are their phone conversations from the road like? The women must resent the whole rock and roll thing at some point—playing music, partying. It's the ultimate Peter Pan life. And women don't like the Peter Pan syndrome. I'm wandering here, I know. But how do you make a relationship work in rock and roll? The other night at a show I stood beside a young blond woman in a long dress. She was pretty, with bare white shoulders and big white teeth. The whole time she stared at Trey on stage with the lustiest look in her eye. Her friends even teased her about it, and she just smiled and kept staring at Trey. I noticed she had an aftershow pass stuck on her dress and she looked very determined.

The Warrior Princess

July 8, Virginia Beach, Virginia

Not sure I'm going to make it to the end. Three more weeks to go, fifteen more shows, and I'm completely worn out after a week on the road. Weary and homesick. Too tired to climb back in the Jimmy. Still feeling dazed from the poison brownie incident. I want my own bed with my girlfriend in it and I want to sit on my back porch and look at the mountains.

Instead I'm poolside at the Super 8 at nine o'clock in the morning, trying to take some notes. Back in the room, Will's on a conference call with some clients. When I left, he was sitting up in bed, a notepad on his lap, talking into his cell phone, "Yeah. . . . Okay. . . . Lehman Brothers are continuing to ramp up on the equity side. . . ." I asked Will what his banker co-workers thought of him going on the Phish tour. "The traders all thought it was pretty fun," he said. "They like to party a lot themselves. They go out, smoke a cigar, drink a lot, pat each other on the back. They're all young and screaming on the phone all day anyways. So they all thought it was really cool. But the more stuffy guys were like, 'You're taking a vacation to do *what?*' They did not understand why that would be fun at all, to drive around, sweaty, on the East Coast, and camp out after a show. With a lot of people there was just a disconnect there, because that was something they would never ever do. I don't think they really even understood what the deal was. Most of the people I work with, in my group anyways, are older. And even most of the guys my age, my roommate, he sort of likes road trips but definitely has the need for something more pampered."

PHOTO COURTESY OF DOUGLASS M. TITUS

Nobody around the pool this morning. Plenty of Phishheads at this motel, but it's early yet. Most don't rise until the maid bangs on the door for housekeeping. Then they roll out of bed, pile into vans, ragged and red-eyed, and take off for the next show. There's a certain biorhythm to this lifestyle. It's almost forced on you. Wake up about noon, never feeling very good, never feeling refreshed or energetic. The afternoons are lazy and long, dragging on in the hot sun, sitting in cramped cars and old vans with no air conditioning, often in terrible traffic jams. At this point—say, about four-thirty p.m., inching along some scorched highway—I think even the most dedicated Phishhead must wonder, "What the fuck am I doing?" They hang their heads out car windows, mouths wide open and eyes half shut, drained by daylight.

But then, at about seven o'clock, an hour or so before the show, a certain kind of energy kicks in. It's hard to describe really, but it's happened to me every night so far on tour, this jump start of adrenaline. Driving to the show, I think, *No, God no, not another one. I'm sick of it all.* . . . Then I step into the arena, the lights dim, and all of a sudden I'm jumping out of my seat waiting for my band to come on stage. *My* band, that's right. You see, when you follow these guys around all over the country, they really become your band. The boys. You know them. After all, you're with them just about every night. The band is just part of the gang, soldiering from arena to arena, night after night.

From about seven to midnight, you're flying, with or without drugs. To tell the truth, it really doesn't matter if you're on anything. Drugs can enhance the experience or completely wreck it (see journal entry for July 5), but in any case, for those four or five hours you literally feed on the music. It makes you move, it makes you dance, it makes you feel happy and full of energy. You feel like you could dance forever. This is the best part of any twenty-four-hour period of life on tour—the "up" part of the biorhythm.

Then the show ends and everyone streams out into the parking lot. There's a little bit of a letdown here, but not much. You're still buzzing from the music, still ready to dance as you walk out of the venue. There are always hundreds, often thousands, of fans who don't get into the show, who never got tickets, never found their miracle, and have wandered around the parking lot doing whatever—buying, selling, smoking, tripping, you name it. In the night, everyone comes alive, inside or outside the show. They holler and dance and beat drums and shake their dreadlocks.

We're stuck in traffic somewhere in Virginia. The sun beats down on the Jimmy. It penetrates the roof. Will doesn't like the AC—says it's bad for his skin. The hot air off the highway drifts through the windows. Every few miles, on the side of the road, we see one of two things: (a) a broken-down VW bus, steam pouring out of the engine, with shirtless Long Hairs milling about trying to fix it, or (b) a bunch of skinny Heads spread-eagle against a cop car, lights flashing. This has become a very familiar sight. We don't even point to it anymore—three dreadlocked dudes, hands on the roof of a cop car, looking over their shoulders at one another. I don't know if they're being pulled over for speeding or what. These old vans don't go very fast. In fact, I don't think I've seen one Phish van traveling over sixty MPH. It's also worth noting that the people spread-eagle on the side of the road are always the Hardcores—i.e., not the preppies in baseball caps driving Hondas. I think the very sight of a skinny dread-locked kid behind the wheel of a VW bus raises the hair on the back of every cop's neck.

With this traffic we probably won't make it to the show before nine o'clock. So far I've only been on time once—Kansas, the first night of the summer tour. Since then I've been chasing these guys across country, always a few hours behind. It's my own fault. We sleep too late, linger at breakfast looking at the map saying, "It's doesn't look so bad today. Why don't we try this route?" We get lost at least once a day.

I have a new respect for people who sell goods on tour. I mean, this tour is nearly impossible just getting from show to show, staring at a shimmering highway for seven, eight hours a day. I cannot comprehend at this point how much organization and energy it would take to make, for example, a hundred cups of fruit salad. Finding ice for the cooler is hard enough. Most gas stations along the tour route are out of ice because it's the first thing that every van load needs.

We pull into a gas station in the middle of nowhere. A tall guy in a tie-dye walks up to me.

"Hey, man," he says. "How far are we?"

"Not sure. I've got a map, though. Where are you coming from?"

"Charlotte. We were at the show last night, but our car caught on fire."

"That one right there?" I say.

"No, dude. Our car caught on fire. It's wrecked."

"Oh."

"We were in the Jacuzzi at the hotel last night after the show. The car was parked there and it was fine. I could see it. It had been turned off for hours. And then we woke up the next morning and it was on fire. So we called up this number, right, and it turned out the car was on fucking *recall*. Some problem with the electrical system. They hooked us up with a rental for the rest of the tour."

"That's good," I say.

"Lost a sleeping bag, man."

"In the fire?"

"Burned right up."

Another guy walks up to us. "Hey, you kids want some acid?" he whispers. He wears transparent sunglasses.

"No," I say. "All set. Thanks, though."

Thanks, though?

It's weird: three total strangers at a farm-country gas station with Phish in common. The tour in common. The road. The heat. Ticket stubs in our back pockets. We're doing the same thing. Part of the same tribe. The guy with the burned car spotted me filling up my tank in dirty tattered shorts, shirtless, and thought: "Phishhead. I'll go and talk to him. See what's up." Then the wild-eyed acid guy saw us—recognized us immediately by our clothes and dress, like spotting your gang's colors—and thought: These dudes might buy some acid.

Commerce is a big part of this tour. It is a necessity. It makes the tour go. Without it, without the daily exchange of goods, there wouldn't be gas money or ticket money. The goods and services—grilled cheese, t-shirts, astrology readings, etc.—are provided by the Hardcores, guys like this acid seller who are on tour for the long haul. The daily injection of cash into this mini-economy comes from the fans going to one or two shows. They flock in like tourists, pick through the parking lot wares, leave behind their twenty-dollar bills, and come away with something native: a glass pipe, a bracelet, a tie-dye. The overwhelming majority of Phish fans are these tourist types—college kids, prep-school kids, yuppies. Age bracket: sixteen–thirty, with the majority in their early twenties. They fuel this economy.

We pull into the Virginia Beach Amphitheater around eight p.m., late again. The scene here is a bit different. A lot of surfer dudes. A lot of very tan, very fit bodies. Each venue seems to have a certain type of Phishhead. In Atlanta it was the southern frat boy with the Sigma something-or-other on a t-shirt. In Kansas it was the wide-eyed midwesterner, not particularly familiar with the whole scene. Tonight the mini-economy will run on the cash of Virginia Beach surfers. There's a very good vibe in the air tonight. Hard to put a finger on really. Something in the air, some bounce. There is a history of good Phish shows in Virginia. For one reason or another, the band seems to like it here and have turned in some of their best shows in Virginia. Like athletes who prefer one arena to another—softer rims, faster ice, etc.—musicians too have favorite places to play. I remember Page telling me on the squash court that his favorite room in the world is Madison Square Garden because when things really get going, you can feel the whole structure of the building shake. The Hampton Coliseum in Virginia, a short drive from here, is another one of those rooms where things just seem to come together for Phish. Last year in November, a few days before Thanksgiving, they did a run at Hampton that has become legendary, a necessary addition to the tape collection. The year before that, the Hampton shows were supposedly even better.

"Hampton looks like a fucking UFO in the middle of a parking lot," Johnny Mac said in Burlington. "It's a great room, really good acoustics. Security is a joke. It's a great venue for psychedelics. All the southern kids just get ripped. Ripped to shit on tons of L and mushrooms. And it's perfect because right across the parking lot there's like fifty motels with lit-up signs a hundred feet in the air, so no matter how spun they get, they can make it back to their hotel, you know."

Walking through the parking lot, Will runs into a friend who works in Washington, D.C. She's come to the show with three other people, all professional types. "We decided at the last minute to take off and we just got here," she said. "It was a four-hour ride."

I fall in behind with one of her friends, a short Asian woman.

"So where are you from?" she says.

"Vermont. How about you?"

"The D.C. area. We just decided to come to the show. We didn't think we were going to make it with the traffic."

"We just pulled in, too," I say.

"Coming from where?"

"Charlotte, North Carolina."

"Oh. What were you doing?"

"There was a show there last night."

"Really? You went to it?"

"Oh, yeah. I'm doing the whole tour, actually."

"Mmm . . . *Whole* thing? . . . Huh . . ."

This is a conversation stopper with this crew. I can see her eyes glaze over, and my guess is she's thinking, *What a loser. The whole tour, my God!* There's definitely a sense among the one-show yuppies that people on tour are either completely addicted to drugs or just totally weird. Why else would anyone do such a thing?

Inside the show we end up behind a few surfer dudes on the floor, maybe ten or fifteen rows back from the stage. One of them still wears his board shorts. Probably came straight from the beach. No shirt. No shoes. He's smoking joint after joint and calling out, "*Yeah*, baby!" about once a minute. He dances sort of like a crab—hunched back, hands snapping the air. Every once in a while he turns around, still dancing, and looks at me and yells, "*Yeah*, baby! You *know* what I'm talking about!" Then he offers me a hit, but there's just no way that's going to happen anytime soon.

Everybody dances at Phish shows. You can generally divide the dancers into two types: the ones who stay by their seats and make do with the tight space, elbow to elbow, and the ones who head for the aisles or the lawn or any open spot where they can dance freely. Nobody really dances with each other. Like you almost never see couples dancing. It's a solo thing. At worst, the dance is disjointed and off-rhythm, either too slow and awkward or too fast and drug-frenzied, sort of maniacal. Will says the Phish dance reminds him of Mr. Jefferson from the TV show *The Jeffersons*. "You know how he had that strut," he says. "That's how they dance."

I don't really understand this.

The best Phish dancers are women, the ones in the aisle who twirl in long dresses.

Between sets I head out to the concessions for a lemonade. (I'm not drinking these days, either.) A young woman pushes through the line, stumbling, her eyes half-shut. "Hey, come on. Take it easy," a few people in line say. She bumps into me and then bumps into the guy next to me and we look at each other and shake our heads.

"That's too much narcotics and alcohol, man," the guy says. He has long blond dreadlocks—the matted, dead-looking kind that take at least a few years to get like that. But his eyes are bright and alert.

"You're right," I said. "Pretty good first set, huh?"

"I liked that 'Fee.' They took it to some different places."

"I missed it. We got to our seats late."

"Dude, what were you doing?"

"I don't know. We've had trouble getting to the shows on time the last few nights. Late start, traffic. Last night I missed 'Loving Cup.'"

"No."

"Yeah," I say, "totally missed it. I could hear it from the parking lot as we pulled in. Page on the grand piano—"

"Dude, you gotta get here on time."

"I know. You're right. Are you doing the rest of the tour?"

"Whole thing. Fall, too. I work for an organic bread company in Chicago and they're okay with me taking off for the tour."

Back inside the show Will strikes up a conversation with Tara from Long Island. We've seen Tara and her husband, Marcus, at the last couple of shows. Both of them have master's degrees and they plan to catch about five shows this summer. On tour, Marcus works on the phone and the Internet. Pulls into the next venue and logs on.

Tara was hooked on the Dead as a kid, ever since her uncle gave her the Dead's *American Beauty*. She saw her first Dead show at fifteen, with a guy from chemistry class, fourth row. When he came to pick her up, he had to step inside and prove to her father that he had a valid driver's license.

Will says he's from San Francisco and that this is his second-ever Phish show.

"Do you know Dark Star?" Tara says.

Dark Star is apparently a Deadhead/Phishhead guru that everyone in the San Francisco Bay area knows.

"No. I don't know him," Will says.

Later, surfing the Phish Web sites—there are thousands and thousands—I happened to come across Marcus and Tara's Web page, with some touring information and plenty of photos of just about anything having to do with Marcus or Tara: graduation photos, grandfather photos, the dates of the wedding and the dates of the rehearsal dinner. You can click for a graphic of Marcus in a karate pose with a fake *GQ* magazine as a backdrop, or you can click for a shot of Tara as Xena the Warrior Princess. Phishheads are incredibly active on the Internet—trading tapes, reviewing shows, posting set lists. It's a way to keep up the community off the tour. The thing that every Web site has in common is long lists of dates: dates of last year's shows, dates of upcoming shows, dates of shows from 1985. Dates, dates, and more dates. It's the link between Phishheads on the Internet, and provides a timeline. Someone looking for a 9/24/88 tape will connect with someone looking for 12/31/98, and a Web relationship springs up. Tape trading among fans has been totally essential in the growth of Phish. Like the Dead, Phish has always allowed fans to record their live shows. And so from the very start, the rap on the band was that the live shows were much better than anything the four guys could produce in the studio. Which just about everyone agrees with, including music critics. I'm not sure Phish would be selling out arenas now without the years and years of tape trading. And Phish fans are serious listeners. They don't sit around and chat with a bootleg on in the background. They sit back and groove.

One fan said, "Their tapes *flew* around the country, and I heard certainly ten, twenty Phish tapes before I ever saw a Phish show."

"Adventurous tapers really do a lot to turn people on to music," Johnny Mac said. "And I'm not saying that Phish fans are the most open musical people in the world, because they're not always, nor were Dead fans. But when they get the tapes and they like it, nobody listens harder."

I get tapes over the Internet from a guy I've never met named Tom. I send him ninety-minute Maxell II's and a SASE ("B&P" in tape-trader terms—blanks and postage). Sometimes he's busy spinning tapes for other people and it takes some time. In the last three years he's spun exactly 134 tapes, at last count. That's a lot of time spinning. But what's amazing is that he knows the exact number. Numbers and dates, the language of tape traders, a language that is a pretty damn weird when you get right down to it.

After the show we head to a KOA campground. The first tent night of the trip. I'm ready to show off my new EMS camping gear to Will, who sort of thinks of himself as Mr. Woodsy since he grew up in Colorado. The last time we went camping together I brought along a sleeping bag I've had since I was a kid. Forest green. The inside was yellow with pictures of deer running through the woods. It was a big sucker, made for sleepovers—indoor temperatures somewhere around seventy degrees. Throughout that night I kept chattering about how can it be this cold in June? And Will kept saying, "We're in the mountains, what did you expect?"

My new stuff seems to impress him.

"Nice tent," he says. "I like the window."

A couple of problems with camping on tour, besides the usual complaints of bugs and bumpy ground. Phishheads scream in the middle of the night. One person, somewhere off in the distance, will holler *"Yeee-haw!"* or something like that. Then the person in the next tent over keeps it going, *"woooo-hoooo!"*—and so on and so on until the whole campground takes part. Periodically, fireworks explode. We can see the flash through the tent window. Then there are the drums. Drums everywhere. They never stop. Tonight we saw a few drummers thumping away and a guy danced around them with fire sticks.

"You think the drums will keep up all night?" Will says at about three a.m.

"Yes."

I hardly sleep. Morning light creeps in through my window flap. Tents as far as you can see. Interspersed among the Phish-

heads, a few vacationing families with little kids are packing up quickly and getting the hell out of here. *What is this?* they must think. *What on earth happened here last night?* I'm sure a few of them wanted to make a fast escape when, past midnight, thousands of these wild hippies in painted buses descended on their campground. But they couldn't have gone anywhere with the narrow roads choked with cars and vans.

Not much activity here yet. RVs wedged between tall trees. Clothes strung out on lines. Dogs roaming freely. Not many leashes on tour, though the dogs seem to be fairly well behaved. No jumping or growling or running wild this morning. It's probably a pretty good life for a dog, doing the tour. Constant company. Always something going on, a grill with an extra veggie burrito, a Frisbee to chase.

A young dreadlocked couple walk by pushing a baby in a stroller. A baby on tour! How awful, right? Well . . . I'm not sure. It's a fairly common sight, babies and toddlers on tour with tie-dyed parents. It's rare, however, that you see a woman alone with a baby on tour, always it seems a mom and a dad. Also, if you're on tour you have a built-in network of friends who are with you all the time and could in theory help out. I bet that some babies on tour get more attention from their parents than babies back in suburbia with professional couples. Seriously, I mean it. Isn't going on tour with your parents, being with them nearly all the time, better than getting left at day care all day?

Party in Underhill

July 9, Columbia, Maryland

The Merriweather Post Pavilion. A strange venue and a bad night. A lot of tension between security and fans. No dancing in the aisles permitted. Security guards in black pants and yellow shirts roamed the show, hauling people off to who knows where. Now it's past midnight, the show's over, and we're stuck in a grumpy crowd leaving the pavilion through one very clogged exit. For some reason we're being herded over a narrow bridge towards the parking lot. Mounted police in combat boots blow whistles. Horseshit everywhere. There's no avoiding it, packed here in the middle of thousands of sweaty, pissed-off fans. We move as one unit: sway to one side, then the other, roll forward a few mini-steps, then back.

It's like the Merriweather security team had a debriefing in the War Room before the show: *"Listen up, we have a situation here."* Which really is ridiculous. Phishheads are probably the most laid-back, nonviolent group of people you'll find anywhere. And all this whip cracking brings out the worst in the fans, many of whom have serious problems with authority in the first place. (Life on the road breeds a fierce independence.) So there's pushing and shouting in this crowd, which rarely happens at Phish shows. I don't feel nervous exactly, but there is an air of tension for the first time on the summer tour.

In the parking lot, the crowd lets off some steam. Fireworks start up. Drums. Music. Dancing. More intense than usual. In one corner, on the edge of the lot near some trees, a series of fireworks blasts into the night and then loud disco cranks through the air from a very large stereo system . . . *Play that funky music, white boy.* . . .

We head over to check it out.

The music comes from the back of a large truck. Somewhere inside the trailer a DJ shuffles around, but it's too dark in there to really see what's going on. These are big speakers, perched on top of tall silver poles. A lot of bass. People are dancing wildly in the grass around the truck. Maybe fifty people. Within minutes, there's more like three hundred people here. It's tough to get a clear look at anyone because a strobe light flashes and clouds of smoke (a dry-ice machine?) drift out of the trailer and float around the field. Nearby, someone has set up a nitrous tank, which is basically laughing gas—it cuts off oxygen to the brain. Five bucks for a balloon full of nitrous. So now everyone's sucking on giant balloons, laughing, screaming, dancing like maniacs, barefoot and shirtless. And the crowd is growing. Everywhere you look thousands of cars, buses, vans, thousands of people all spilling out of the arena, out into the night. . . . Usually once a day on tour I have this thought: How did this ever get so big? Phish, their fans, all of it . . . ?

From the early days, wild outdoor parties have been part of the Phish scene. One of the more popular tapes that circulates among fans is a show from 1988 at Pete Danforth's house in Underhill, Vermont. Pete's parents were out of town for a while, so he threw a rager. Eight hundred people showed up on a July evening and Phish played until three a.m.

Looking for Pete, I called the Danforths' house in Underhill.

A man answered the phone. "Dr. Danforth," he said.

I asked for Pete's number.

Dr. Danforth asked if I was a friend. I started to explain about the book and he interrupted me.

"So you must have heard about the concert out here," he said.

"Yeah."

"My wife and I were on sabbatical leave in Switzerland," he said, "and we got a call from our neighbor saying, 'Do you know what's going on at your house?' Pete had planned this thing without giving much thought to the crowds that would show up. There were cars parked all over the field."

I expected Dr. Danforth to be pissed. You know, still steaming about the whole thing ten years later. But he wasn't. He seemed psyched about it—talked about how it was a good show supposedly, and had I heard the tape?

We hung up and I called his son, Pete, who works for an organic food store in Stowe and plays saxophone in a band called Sic, which makes the local bar rounds.

I asked Pete where the idea for the party came from.

"I knew the guys from seeing shows at Nectar's," Pete said. "One day I was talking to Trey when he was playing guitar at a coffee shop in town, in Burlington. I said my folks were going away for a bit and he said, 'Well, can we play at your place?' I said sure. Basically we had them play on the back porch, overlooking a pond and a field with a semicircle of trees providing a natural amphitheatre. The trees provided really good acoustics."

Pete Danforth paid Phish four hundred dollars and charged three bucks per carload. He turned in a nice profit. The twelve kegs were kicked before the night really took off. It rained for a while, and then when the rain cleared Phish started to play. "I got a lot more people than I thought," Pete said. "It was pretty insane. There were a lot of naked people running around and swimming and running around the woods. There was a bonfire. I got to get up and play for a few songs. I play saxophone. My favorite part was 'Slave to the Traffic Light.' Then they asked me back up to play 'Fire' by Jimi Hendrix, and that didn't go so well."

In the last five years, Pete's only been to a few shows. Like a lot of fans from the old days, he doesn't travel far and wide to see the band anymore.

I asked him if he's surprised at how big they are now.

"I knew they were going to be big back in '86," Pete said. "Even when there were ten people at Nectar's."

Escape from New Jersey

July 10, Camden, New Jersey

Carloads of grumpy Phishheads this morning outside the Super 8 Motel, swearing they'll never come back to Merriweather again. They trade stories from last night and go about the morning routine of cleaning out the van, collecting beer bottles, draining coolers. Most Phishheads keep a pretty well-organized vehicle: pots and pans in order, sleeping bags rolled up and stacked, bong tucked away under the seat. One thing about life on the road is that you have a lot of time on your hands for chores like this. Organizing the van is the perfect task: doesn't require much energy and you can listen to tunes while you work.

Nobody moves very quickly this morning. But nobody on tour moves quickly at any time of the day. Everything happens at a kind of half-speed. People don't drive as fast, they don't honk in traffic, they don't complain waiting on line for the Porta Potty. You have to be patient on tour because life on the road can be a huge pain in the ass—gridlock before and after every show, no escape from the heat, car trouble, long lines for food and water. Your average day on tour is full of many such annoyances, things completely out of your control, the kind of things that if they happened to you back in normal life you'd say, "I'm having a bad day." But on tour the attitude seems to be, "We'll get there. Don't sweat it."

The music itself demands a certain kind of patience. Phish doesn't get up there and play four-minute pop songs. They'll play a song for twenty minutes, often with no lyrics, just one big jam. Most people get antsy with this kind of music. If you play a

Phish bootleg for someone for the first time they usually grow
weary of it after a few minutes, or they'll just start talking and
ignore the music, or they'll say something lukewarm: "I bet
they'd be good live." The music doesn't have immediate appeal
for most people who want to "get it" right away. It doesn't happen that way. You have to stick around a while, let the music
develop.

We're packing up in a rush this morning at the Super 8. No
lingering over HBO or dawdling in the motel lobby. No
half-speed for us.

"Chop, chop," Will says. "I want to make it on time tonight. I
want to check out the parking lot scene."

"Fine."

"And we won't get lost today. I already looked at the map. It's
an easy drive. Let's go."

"If you get a speeding ticket, don't tell him we're going to a
Phish show. Don't mention anything about Phish."

We walk across the street to a diner. There's a jukebox playing
oldies and the place is full of Phishheads, of course. We drop in
some quarters and choose a few songs. Everyone looks a bit dazed
and tired, staring out the window at the parking lot with the
music floating in the background . . . *Bye bye love/Bye bye hap-
piness.* . . . The waitress walks by with a quick step, armful of hot
plates, singing along to the jukebox. She's the only bright spot in
here. The only person smiling and, it seems, the only person talking. My God, a weary morning on the summer tour. Everyone
looks sick of it all. Another day, another drive, another shimmering highway. Tonight's show feels like a year away.

"If it came easy, everyone would do it," Johnny Mac said back
in Burlington. "The whole idea is that the journey is at least as
interesting as the destination. You're not going to drive to Kansas
City in the summer otherwise. It's like when you're in the army
or summer camp or anything like that, there really is this bond
that you form when you are under these unusual circumstances.

And it doesn't necessarily have to last your whole life and all that, but it's great. There is a sort of camaraderie. You know, a friend of mine was joking, he said it was like summer camp with drugs. It really is. You see the same faces. There are a lot of people that normally you wouldn't relate to. You're meeting a generation of people.

"The road has a lot of appeal. It's the hero's journey, you know. In like the Campbell sense. Joseph Campbell. *The Hero of a Thousand Faces.* You go out on the road not knowing what to expect. You have all these expectations. You turn the key in your car and you drive or you hitch or get a ride with somebody, you get on a bus and all of a sudden everything you expected doesn't happen. All your expectations aren't met. In some ways they're surpassed and in some ways they're let down."

The waitress comes back with our food, singing as she puts the plates down . . . *And it burns burns burns/The ring of fire. . . .* She's too young to be working in a place like this, singing Johnny Cash. I try to brighten things up a bit with Marvin Gaye's "Let's Get It On," but as I'm pushing the buttons Will makes a face.

"You want to hear 'Let's Get It On' on a Saturday morning?"

"Yeah. . . . What? Too sexy?"

"Definitely. Especially for two guys hanging out together."

On the way out we walk by a group of Phishheads piling out of a Winnebago. The smell of patchouli drifts across the parking lot.

"Hey," one of them says, "I hear you can smoke weed in this diner."

On the highway we get lost. Some bridge confusion. I take the blame. ("I pride myself on not getting lost," Will says.) By three o'clock we're in the parking lot, drinking Coors Light and tossing the Nerf football. Camden, New Jersey, is an ugly place, a deserted, crumbling city. Doesn't look very safe, either. The parking lot for the E Centre (short for the Sony Blockbuster Entertainment Centre—all the pavilions have corporate names now) butts up against the Jersey River and looks across the brown water at downtown Philadelphia. We park beneath a big rum-

bling bridge and pretty soon we have another guy joining us in
our game of football. He's tall and wears sandals. He runs deep
patterns and leaps for the ball when it's out of reach, not worrying so much about who's in the way. He's really into it. I can
throw a Nerf far, and I launch bomb after bomb over the crowd of
people walking by, and this guy chases them down, sometimes
catching the ball, sometimes not. It's windy by the river and the
football hangs up there wobbly and curving to the left. It blows
clear across our row, over the vans and into another row, and the
guy sprints through the crowd looking up at the sky. This is one
of my favorite things at a Phish show—throwing a football in the
parking lot. Everyone's walking around and feeling pretty good
on a summer afternoon with the show a few hours away. People
sit on top of Winnebagos watching the crowd pass by. This is
something I want to do at some point—sit on top of a Winnebago
in a lawn chair. That would be the way to do the tour: in a Winnebago with a small kitchen, a few beds, a bathroom, a loud
stereo, and a ladder on the back leading to the roof.

By about five p.m. things are really rolling here. To our left, in
the next space over, two guys are launching fireworks, M-80's in
particular. They've been drinking Heineken tall boys all afternoon. Whenever we hear one of them shout "Fire in the hole!"
we duck inside the Jimmy and wait for the explosion.

Across from us, in the backseat of a Pontiac Grand Am, a
young couple is having sex. I can see it.

"Go check it out," I say to Will.

"No, why don't you?"

"Because she saw me earlier looking at them. It'd be weird if I
went. Just walk by and circle back around."

Which he does. A quick glance in the side window confirms
everything.

"They are *definitely* having sex," Will says after his little stroll.

"What did you see?"

"Not much. But enough to know."

I can see plenty from here. She's riding up and down, facing the back window, her arms around his neck and her long blond hair swishing around. She keeps her shirt on. She glances up every once in a while and I think she knows I'm watching. But I keep looking back, of course. How could you not? It turns into a marathon session. Different positions, one after the other, some of which are hard to figure out because you only see a shoulder or a knee or a flash of blond hair. No one else notices them. People walk by every second and no one thinks to take a look at the Grand Am. Our angle of vision from the back of the Jimmy is perfect.

"Fire in the hole!"

We scramble inside.

"There's a lot of shit going on here," Will says, curled up against the cooler.

"You're right."

A short-haired man in a green polo shirt, about thirty-five, walks past us, glancing around suspiciously. He has a wire in his ear. He turns and heads back in our direction.

"Narc," I say. "Check him out."

The narc stops for a moment, puts a finger to his ear, and talks into this collar. Probably FBI.

"Yeah," Will says. "There's another one." He points to another guy with an earpiece. Then the two earpiece guys converse with a small bearded man who carries a huge backpack. He walks in a stoop and seems to be in pain. The three of them move towards us and huddle between the Jimmy and the M-80 car, which still reeks of gunpowder.

"What the hell are they doing?" Will whispers.

"I don't know. Don't turn around."

"Why did they—"

"We got nothing to hide," I say. "Forget it. I think it's some kind of stinger operation."

One of them says, "You listen to me and don't listen to anyone else. Got that?"

I hear some rustling, a zipper, and a clanking sound as they haul out whatever was in the backpack. Then all of a sudden I hear the M-80 guy grumbling about something, his speech slurred from an afternoon of Heinekens. His voice is too loud. He's done, I think to myself. Might as well arrest him now for possession of illegal explosives.

"Hey, man," M-80 says, "don't set up here. I don't want trouble."

At this point we both turn around and see a big silver tank shaped like a missile. Nitrous. These guys aren't narcs. They're drug dealers. Nitrous runners who stand to make thousands and thousands of dollars today if they can keep a low profile and elude the cops. They take one look at M-80—wobbly on his feet, waving a half-drunk Heineken tall boy—and decide to pack up immediately.

"Let's move out," the one in charge says. In a few seconds they're gone, the short guy with the tank strapped to his back struggling with each step.

A couple of problems running nitrous at a Phish show in broad daylight: (1) A working nitrous tank makes a distinct noise, a long hiss, like a loud gas station air pump. This sound travels over a pretty good distance and can attract the attention of police. (2) A long line forms whenever a tank opens for business—a hundred or so people in single file, another hundred wandering off, one by one, with giant balloons. Of course, this too attracts a cop's eye. So nitrous runners are literally on the move. They set up shop for a while and then hit the road, relocate on the other side of the parking lot. A shrewd tank operator knows when it's time to close down for a few minutes. He senses a bad scene—a big crowd, a long line, a noisy group of laughing Phishheads.

The trio with the ear equipment opens for business a few cars away. These dudes are *organized*. Two of them work the tank, filling balloons and collecting money, and the third keeps an eye out for cops. He paces nervously and surveys the scene standing on the bumper of a jeep. He appears to be the One in Charge, talking

into his turned-up collar to his spotters, who are positioned around the parking lot keeping track of police movement. There are two spotters, as far as we can tell, bringing the team total to five. Once in a while the spotters stroll into view. Both about fifty years old, fat, wearing tank tops. One of them scratches his crotch frequently and is easily spooked. The other, tougher and fatter, says, quite loudly into his collar, "*That's* what I'm fucking talking about." Which seems strange to people passing by, a fifty-year-old man in a tank top talking to no one.

"You should get a picture of one of these guys," Will says.

"Yeah . . . but . . . look at them. They won't like it if they see me with a camera pointing in their direction."

"Here, take the camera and I'll go stand in the street. You can pretend to be taking a picture of me."

I get Will in the frame, and then Tank Top settles into the background, a little bit blurry, but still I can tell through the lens that he's very antsy, suspicious, and that he wouldn't like this photo at all.

The cops stand no chance against this nitrous team. They are way out of their league, patrolling the parking lot on bikes. They pedal through the crowd leisurely. They don't even split up. Just one pack of spandexed bike cops talking among each other and traveling about five MPH. You could set a clock to their laps through here. Not very hard work for the spotters.

"You know," Will says, leaning on the back of the Jimmy, "I can see how someone could get used to this life. Never a dull moment. Always something going on. A party each night."

A chilly breeze comes off the river after the show. In the dark this place is sinister. The nasty hiss of nitrous tanks everywhere, wild laughing. Phishheads like skinny ghosts float by, grinning, the red and green balloons bobbing in the night. The partying has reached a new level and the cops have completely given up in here. There's new competition now for the nitrous business. A couple of guys with small tanks have opened up on their own. No spotters necessary. Five bucks a balloon. A half hour of brisk sales could pay your way the rest of the tour.*

Massive traffic jam in the parking lot. The few cars trying to make a quick postshow getaway aren't going anywhere. Most people don't even try to pull out of their space.

"I'm going to get some food," I say to Will. "Do you want anything?"

"What are you going to get?"

"I don't know. Grilled cheese. Burrito. I'll find something."

"I think who you buy from all depends on what the person looks like, how skinny or desperate. Some guys you just don't want to buy anything from."

---

*A nitrous tank is supposedly not that expensive if you know where to get it. Later on I heard about one dealer's routine: He goes down to Boston carrying a fake company ID with a fake account and a fake driver's license. He walks into a back alley and pays $150 for a five-foot nitrous tank. He thinks the place he buys it from is mafia-run, though he doesn't ask any questions. And they won't help him carry the tank out of the alley—that's part of the deal. A five-foot tank can fill up about four hundred balloons, so you can imagine how much money you stand to make if you run a few tanks.

"So do you want something?"

"Sure. Whatever you get."

I head towards the lights and music in the far corner of the parking lot. At every Phish show there is a busy section of business called Shakedown Street, a leftover term from the Grateful Dead days. RVs and vans line each side of Shakedown Street and the owners set up shop outside their vehicles. It's sort of like being at a fair. On Shakedown Street you can buy just about anything. The food vendors make the most money and their busiest time is about midnight, after the show lets out.

"Bad ass egg rolls, two dollars."

"Phatty burritos, three bucks. Two for five."

"Who's thirsty? I got your Sammy Smith."

"Shrooms. Who needs them?" A little guy in a hooded sweatshirt weaves through the crowd. "Who needs some shrooms?"

The food is pretty good. Mostly vegetarian. Phishheads as a group seem to be strictly vegetarian, but I've seen plenty of fans inside the concert venue chomping on five-dollar hot dogs. You won't find a hot dog on Shakedown Street. The people selling other goods—t-shirts, bracelets, pipes—don't fare quite as well. They usually spread their wares out on a blanket and sit beside them quietly. Compared to the food vendors, they are terrible salesmen.

Usually what happens with the food is one place will get hot. It starts with a few people waiting in line beside a grill and then other people walking down Shakedown Street see the line and come over to check it out. Pretty soon one raggedy young couple flipping falafels on a small gas stove has more orders than they can handle. I've stood in line before waiting for I don't know what, when some perfectly respectable-looking guy with no business was shouting, "Tastee Burritos! Only a buck!"

I buy two cheese quesadillas from a woman with long braids and head back to the Jimmy. This place is out of control: bottle rockets whizzing by, people skipping along with a balloon in each hand, screaming into the night, taking a hit of nitrous, screaming some more. Every other person looks completely crazy, like they've lost all control. Drums everywhere, people dancing on broken glass. It reminds me of the movie *Escape from New York*, where the whole island of Manhattan is transformed into a penal colony. Once you were sent to the island, all rules were off: no laws, no police, no prison guards. You had the run of the place but could never leave. I haven't seen the movie since I was a kid. It scared the crap out of me. Wild-eyed criminals in tattered clothes running around New York City in the dark. One of the criminals was named Hyena, I think because of his wicked laugh. He was just about the creepiest thing I'd ever seen. Tonight I've spotted about a dozen people who are dead ringers for Hyena.

When I get back to the Jimmy I ask Will if I've missed anything.

"You missed a fight between one of the nitrous guys and a customer."

"What happened?"

"I don't know really what it was about. The nitrous guy started choking him. I think it was over money. Not sure, though. They both looked pretty high, actually. The nitrous guy flipped out, jumped on top of him and started swinging. It was pretty bad. And then it just stopped. I think the nitrous guy realized he was losing money."

A loud *thunk!* from the next car over. A small, long-haired man with a balloon falls down and bounces off the car's hood on the way. His friends circle around him.

"That's the other thing," Will says. "A lot of people seem to be falling head first or tumbling over backwards. They don't put their hands out when they fall."

"Double-fisting the balloon."

"Yeah," he says. "You know, this is insane. I can't believe how loud these tanks are. It sounds like a runway. An airport runway—you know, the hissing."

"You're right."

"Oh, you also missed Noah. He finally made a few sales after a massive markdown. He sold shirts for five bucks."

All afternoon Noah was sitting across from us, beside the gently rocking Pontiac Grand Am, with a display of ugly tie-dyes hanging off the back of his car. Beside the shirts a colorful poster read, WE'RE TAKING A STAND AGAINST CORPORATE AMERICA. Noah was tall and skinny and very serious, with a big curly bush of hair on top of a little head. His girlfriend, who looked sort of the same, sold baggy dresses. All afternoon not one sale. At some point Noah came over and introduced himself, bell-bottoms dragging on the ground. "Hi, I'm Noah. . . ." He was sober and intense. His eyes darted around, studying the scene. He and his girlfriend are typical of a certain kind of couple on tour: very earnest, very young, maybe twenty, and full of misguided energy. They know every lyric to every Phish song, can tell you the entire set list for last fall's show in Mountain View, California, will announce how many shows they've been to—total, including today—and they will, if you stick around, lay out their entire touring itinerary.

Noah walks back to his car now. In the dark the first thing you see is an armful of tie-dyes. Apparently he's taken his t-shirts on the road. I can't believe that anyone's buying shirts now, at two A.M., in all this chaos. The M-80 guys show up. They look terrible. Like zombies. One of them stumbles on an empty Heineken.

"Hey, what's up?" I say.

Neither of them recognize me. They climb into their car and pass out. The Grand Am couple returns—Baggy Shorts and Tight Jeans. They've locked the key in the Pontiac. After a big fight, they storm off in different directions.

Middle-aged men push grocery carts through the mess, collecting cans and bottles. They move slowly and look tired.

For hours now the traffic in the parking lot hasn't moved.

"I better confirm our motel reservation," I say at about three a.m. "They may have a late check-in policy."

Will hands me his cell phone.

"I'm sorry, sir," the woman on the line says. "Your credit card was rejected. We couldn't hold your room."

"That's not possible."

"We tried it twice, sir. We have nothing left tonight."

Will lies down in the backseat. "Why don't we just sleep here? We won't get out of the parking lot for another few hours anyway. Lock up the Jimmy."

Neither of us falls asleep. The fireworks. The shattering bottles. The hissing. And the disco music. Phishheads love disco music late at night. The best stereo systems are exclusively disco. Donna Summer, the Bee Gees, Kool and the Gang, you name it.

The cops drive through at about four a.m. "Clear out!" they bark through a fuzzy loudspeaker. "The parking lot is closing in fifteen minutes! Clear out!" The tires crunch slowly on the acres of broken glass. No one budges. The disco RV with the swirling colored lights turns down the music for a few seconds. The cops move on, the music cranks back up: *Macho macho man*. . . .

Get on the Bus

July 11, Burlington, Vermont

Back in the mountains for a day and a half of rest and recovery. Thank God. Not sure I'm ever going to leave. Town is quiet with no students around, especially the college section of town— empty sidewalks, empty porches, no couches on the lawns, no tapestries in the windows, no one running around at three a.m. shouting about this or that, no blond girls in jeeps with navy Connecticut license plates. But it's only mid-July, early yet. In a few weeks they'll start pouring in, well before school starts. Students seem to come back especially early, just as August gets rolling. And why not? Can't you picture it—a twenty-year-old kid mowing lawns in a New Jersey suburb, thinking, Damn, I can't wait to get back to Burlington. Whenever *Playboy* or *Rolling Stone* comes out with a list of the top party schools in the nation, UVM is always up there, battling it out with schools like Arizona State and Florida, and there's always a quote from a UVM kid named Travis or Trevor saying something like, "It's because of the long winters." I think UVM is one of the only schools in New England left with fraternities. About once a year the local paper explodes with stories about some sort of hazing disaster. Or there will be a study on alcohol abuse at the college, and the president or dean of students will make a promise in print to form a committee to look into the problem immediately. But all this is on the other side of July. For now, for a very short period, the sun burns in a blue sky and you can park wherever you want and sleep with your windows wide open.

Around Christmas, town empties out again. College kids head home for break and a good chunk of the bar scene departs for the New Year's Phish shows, usually in New York or Boston. It seems like half the town gets free tickets. From the start, Phish has been very generous with comp tickets and aftershow passes—hundreds of tickets given away each show, and for New Year's it reaches over a thousand. At any Phish show you go to, especially in the Northeast, there's a whole section of Burlington people with the best seats in the house. Every show I go to—Kansas, Virginia, anywhere—I recognize people from around town. And that's how it's always been, from the very first time these four guys left Vermont to play their first semi-big-deal club—the Paradise in Boston. Thinking Phish wasn't worth their time, the Paradise refused to offer them a night. Fine, the band said, we'll rent the place out and bring our own fans. Busloads of Burlington fans made the trip to see Phish sell out the Paradise.

Tom Baggot, now a booking agent in Atlanta, was a UVM student in the late eighties and helped organize the bus trip. "A guy named Brother Craig and myself organized it," Tom said. "We got these old buses, forty-six-seat Bluebird buses. We just sold tickets to our friends. It wasn't advertised, you know. All word of mouth. People who knew *knew*. We hyped it up: 'Phish has got to sell out the Paradise—let's go!' The bus driver didn't care what was going on. We partied hard on the buses. I remember at the club overhearing this talent agent say, 'I don't understand—I wouldn't rent the room out and they sold it out.' It was by any standard a fantastic night."

Tom came to Burlington as a freshman in the fall of 1987, just as Phish was beginning to pack Nectar's on Main Street. "I remember some of the very first Phish shows that attracted a hundred or so people," he said. "It was the early fall of '87 and there was a new crop of freshmen at UVM. First there were forty people, then eighty people, then two hundred. Nectar's took the tables out. There was a solid hundred of us from that one class, kids that had been turned on to the Dead and were looking for something more mainstream, more irreverent, more zany. It was pretty much in that fall that a microcosm of the scene started to form. Pot-smoking, longhaired hippie-freaker types and also middle-class intelligent kids. There was a disproportionate number that fall of kids who just fell for the band and that became a nucleus that kept growing and growing. It was a phenomenon from the start. The first time I saw the band, as bad as they were, I knew they were going to be something serious. They were passionate. They were young, working out their instruments, but they were full speed ahead—you know, 'run like an antelope.' People saw that and caught on immediately. I spun tapes and gave them to people. I was a proselytizer. I was a diehard fan for years and years and did everything I could to spread Phish."

Ian McLain is another fan from the early days. He lives in the sticks outside of Burlington ("Forty minutes from Nectar's," he says) in a house he built himself at the end of a dirt road. The drive out to Ian's place is like a lot of drives through Vermont— twisty roads through a rolling, open landscape with trees and barns scattered about. Old graveyards with tilting headstones, thin and white, by the side of the road. Red barns collapsing and rotting and somehow holding together with age. Grain silos here and there, a farmhouse, an old tractor. Not many cars pass you on these roads. The landscape just rolls along and everything is quiet. Every ten or so miles you pass through a small town with a few dozen houses, a church with a white steeple, and a convenience store where there's usually a couple of trucks parked outside, engines running, and an old man working the register in a plaid shirt. There's a few mobile homes, a few nice homes, some rusty cars, and then *boom*, you're back out into the country rolling along again. In the winter the landscape is bare and lonely, sometimes brown, sometimes white. At night, in the winter, with a moon in the sky and the land and hills around you glowing, that sight through my car window gives me the shivers. In the spring the land explodes with green and mosquitoes and every possible form of tiny life buzzes in the air. In the fall the leaves change, and I suppose if there were a heaven on earth they would construct it very much like Vermont.

Ian McLain's property in the foothills of the Green Mountains is patrolled by German shepherds. He trains dogs for police work, and at any one time there are maybe six or seven shepherds pacing behind fences as you pull up the driveway, and each one of those mothers will keep you in your car, doors locked, until Ian comes out and waves you in. Like a lot of Vermonters, Ian juggles a bunch of jobs, and his work depends on the season—carpenter in the summer, ski patrol in the winter. The dog training alone doesn't pay the bills. He's thirty-eight now and still goes to Phish shows.

"I really do love the fucking music still," Ian said. "It still rocks me. It can really rock my world sometimes. When I'm taken away by the music and I close my eyes and I don't think about the two hours it took me to get there or the guy who spilled beer on me. When I hear the band play now, it's still the same basic music, you know. When I close my eyes and I'm at the show, at the Garden, to me more of my memory of Phish is at Nectar's or at a little bar or at someone's house or at my place or in Eric's* living room, because the music still sounds the same, and if I close my eyes I can just be there."

Part of the reason I've come out here is to hear about a couple of shows that Phish played nearly fifteen years ago at Ian's farm in Hebron, New York, just over the Vermont border. The tapes of those shows are staples in any serious fan's collection.

I asked Ian what the farm was like.

"It was a total redneck scene. We'd drink beer and throw the cans off the porch and shoot guns into the woods. I lived with my friend Woody, and he hunted a lot, and we were living the redneck country lifestyle. The first time they played at my house,

---

*Eric is another old-schooler who is now on the Phish payroll as the band's masseur, traveling with them everywhere they go and giving the band members daily rubdowns.

which is a pretty famous tape—a lot of people have that one—
there was only like fifty people there. There was drug dealers
from New York City and crazy people from over in southern
Vermont and—you know, just a bunch of wackos all converging.
People hadn't heard of Phish at all. They were still like a garage
band from Burlington. It was pretty wild. I remember all the
dogs barking. There must have been a hundred dog barks. At the
party there was probably fifteen dogs running around barking to
the music. But they just kept on playing. Hours. By the time they
stopped playing, nobody was paying any attention. There was
like three people at the keg and one guy chasing a dog around the
yard and they were just staring off into outer space and playing.
Pretty cool."

Ian and his buddies started making regular trips to Nectar's.

"They had a following," Ian said. "We all wanted to go see
Phish at Nectar's. We were definitely way into the band by '87.
The guys I hung out with were all big Deadheads, too. By the
time the late eighties came, we were like, 'To hell with the
Dead—these guys jam way harder.' They could bring us places
the Dead couldn't anymore. Jerry was a junkie and they were
playing really standard sets. We'd go see Phish and they could
bring you out to la-la land and back, many times."

"When did you think that they could really make it?" I said.

"When I knew they were going to make it was when I was
getting a sandwich at Tinguini's, which was a sandwich shop on
Shelburne Road where Jiffy Lube is now. Page was the sandwich
guy at Tinguini's. And we got into a conversation and I was bust-
ing his balls back there—'Sandwich Boy' or something—and he
said, 'Hey, man, this is totally short-term. I'm going to be a musician. I'm a musician. This is paying my way to being a musician.'
He knew it then, he was going to be a musician."

"Did you believe him, or did you think he was dreaming?"

"I thought, Good luck, man—he's cocky and he'll end up making it. Needless to say, he probably quit Tinguini's within six
months and was on the road."

Hawaiian Creepers

July 13, Great Woods, Massachusetts

The Great Woods scene is a lot of prep school kids running around in baseball caps. Choate, Milton, Exeter t-shirts everywhere you look. Not many of the Hardcores on tour make it into Great Woods. There are so many kids in the Boston area who snatch up the tickets as soon as they go on sale that a lot of the traveling Phishheads get boxed out. The same will be true for the New Jersey shows later this week—swarmed by suburban teenagers. I talked to a couple of Phishheads somewhere along the way, maybe Atlanta, who said they were going to skip this leg of the tour and instead travel to some bluegrass festival and then rejoin the tour after New Jersey.

Between sets a spaced-out teenager in a baggy sweatshirt starts talking to me. I'm sitting on a railing near a concession stand, eating a big salty pretzel.

"Hey, what's up, man?" he says. "Great night tonight, huh? It's perfect, really just *perfect*. Don't you think? *Perfect*."

"Sure is," I say.

"It's just so nice. The trees are so *green*—look at them." He points at the trees. "So *green*. And the sky—look at the sky, look at it. Everything is perfect."

"Yeah."

"Look around. Isn't it awesome?"

"Well, yeah—"

"Are you cold, man? I'm hot. I'm not cold. Hey, my name's Happy."

"Happy?"

"Yeah. Happy. I've been on the whole tour, man. I hitchhiked from Ohio to Kansas and it took me four days, man. Not three or two days, I thought it would take that, but four days, man. *Four* days."

"Four days?"

"Yeah, man. That's what I'm talking about. Isn't it great tonight?"

"Who picked you up?"

"These people going to Kansas, man. They were *awesome*! Are you having a good night, 'cause I'm having a great night! Look at the *trees*!"

"What are you on right now?"

"Me? Nothing, man. Nothing."

"Seriously, what are you on?"

"*Nothing*, man. It's just the way I am."

"That's not possible."

"It's true. It's me."

After a minute, Happy shakes my hand and walks off.

Now is probably a good time to mention a letter I got from my friend Liam, who followed Phish around Europe last summer in a black Mercedes. Before the big trip, he'd never been to a show. He was already in England at the time, studying at Cambridge, and so when a few friends from the U.S. came over to follow Phish, Liam decided to join them. On the phone I heard about the trip in bits and pieces—something about a mysterious rash and a late night in the ER. The rash he picked up in Barcelona, though he's not sure exactly, and it covered his face and chest and back. Another guy in the black Mercedes came down with it, too. The rash, the drugs, all of it, the whole trip, it was too much for Liam. He wasn't prepared. The Mercedes crew stashed mushrooms in bottles of Ragù tomato sauce for the border crossing—specifically, Hawaiian Creepers, a type of mushroom which Liam found incredibly powerful and really couldn't even describe. Along the way they slept in the car and crashed with friends in hotels. One of the highlights was floating around the pool of a five-star hotel with a guy named Harry. I know Harry from college, though he never seems to recognize me. I run into Harry a lot at Phish shows—Dead shows before that. I always go up and say hi and he always looks at me with a confused expression. Harry apparently traveled the Europe summer tour in style. "Harry went first-class," Liam wrote. "His place in Amsterdam had three rooms with black leather couches and a balcony. His place in Barcelona had a pool with a waiter who served drinks. We bathed there. Each place Harry stayed in looked as if he'd lived there for months."

A quick aside: While following Phish, Liam ran into Shack in Prague. Shack was in Europe for the World Cup soccer, attending games in full red-white-and-blue body paint. With a cape. Shack was in rough shape, however, according to Liam—heading back to the hotel early while everyone else stayed out, vexed by the same problem of binding up in the bathroom. The group Shack was traveling with didn't make it easier. They would gather round the bathroom whenever he grimly shut the door behind him to try again. At which point they would clap and chant, call out his name, cheer him on, wait and wait and wait for news.

Anyway . . . moving on . . . Liam isn't much of a Phish fan. So I e-mailed Hayden, another guy in the black Mercedes, and asked him about the tour. Unlike Liam, who really has no interest in Phish, Hayden is a huge fan who has been to well over a hundred shows. He e-mailed me back:

Christiana in Copenhagen was probably the coolest place I have ever and will ever see a show. It was so small and intimate, and everything was legal! The band was just milling around in the beer garden before the show, talking to fans, getting a buzz on. It was all so fantastic. The first set of the first night was so hot. Three tunes had been totally reworked (ghost, water in the sky and moma dance), and, up to that point, never been played live. Everything about the trip was out of control. It totally threw Liam for a loop, because everything was pretty unpredictable, due to the level we would take it to every time they played.

At one point on the trip, in Prague, they lost their friend Beach. He disappeared without a trace, Hayden said, and so they went to a Czech police station to file a missing persons report, which station Hayden described as very "Eastern bloc" with interrogation rooms and an "antechamber." Later they found Beach walking down the street.

Apparently Hayden never got the rash that Liam and Beach came down with. He said it caused some tension on the trip because he wouldn't go near them once they broke out and refused to touch anything they had touched. Hayden thinks they picked it up in the Netherlands, but in any case he kept his distance, and in the meantime met a Polish girl named Agata. They hung out on the Mediterranean shore, smoking cigarettes and sipping drinks before the show, while Liam and Beach departed for the emergency room.

Run Like an Antelope

July 15, Holmdel, New Jersey

The more I see Phish, the more I want to see them. You'd think it would be just the opposite—that you'd get sick of it after a while. Same music, same band, same songs. But I've become even more of a fan on tour. I'm sick of crisscrossing the country on these terrible highways, and yet the show itself never gets old. And each night is different. It's like the more you see the Yankees play at the stadium, the more devoted you become and the more you want to keep going *back* to the stadium. You notice the way the shortstop pulls on his cap before he crouches, or the way the right fielder gazes out into the bleachers between pitches. You don't know what's going to happen night to night, but certain things are very familiar because you've been there before. You have a stake in what's happening. That's why fanatics develop on an escalating scale—the more you're a part of it, the bigger a fanatic you become.

One of the appealing things about life on the road with Phish is that it forces you to enjoy the moment. At the show, you don't think about the next day or next week. You see all these people dancing around in dirty bare feet, the music pouring over you, everybody sweating, and you think, There's nowhere else I'd rather be right now. Where else do you get this feeling? We're all so busy day to day, running around doing this, doing that, hustling here, hustling there. When do you stop and just suck up everything around you? I suppose you might say, Well, I appreciate the sunset once in a while or a really good meal or a walk in the woods. That's fine. But I'm talking about a celebration with thousands of dancing maniacs, all caught up in the frenzy of the music, all experiencing the same thing at the same time. A Phish tune called "Run Like an Antelope" captures the frenzy of it all, the celebration. Of course, this sort of thing you can't capture in writing, words on a page simply can't do it, but, well . . . the song is one long jam, building up, faster and faster, hardly any lyrics until the very end, totally frenetic:

> Run run run run run run run run run run run run . . .
> Run run run run run run run run run run run run . . .
> You've got to run like an antelope out of control
> You've got to run like an antelope out of control
> Run like an antelope out of control
> Run like an antelope out of control . . .

At this point you're really moving. I mean, you can barely keep up with their pace. You feel like a goddamn antelope. Antelopes are fast mothers. Drenched in sweat, loose, limby, you can dance better than you ever thought you could. Really groovin', rubbery. And you're not dancing *with* anybody in particular. No partner to account for, so you can let it rip. In this moment at a show there's almost nothing in the world I'd rather be doing. And here's the strange part, the thing that has surprised me: with each show, I become more absorbed into the music. I dance harder. I didn't expect this to happen. A month ago I thought, Well, I'll hit the road and write this book, hear some great stories, and no matter what, living on the road will be exciting. I thought the trip itself would be the highlight and the music would just sort of be there night after night. It's turned out to be just the opposite. The music is what makes it all worth it.

When I saw my first Phish show five years ago, I remember thinking, Now *this* is different, all this wild dancing. People danced at Dead shows, of course. It was a big part of the experience. But this "Run like an antelope" crap—what the hell is going on? I thought. I liked it. But I certainly wasn't doing the antelope right away. A part of me immediately responded to it. Another part thought, This is sort of goofy. Like I found it very strange that at certain points in the show each band member played his instrument as fast as he possibly could, barely holding it together, and that this more than anything sent the crowd into a fit. I hadn't seen this before at other concerts. I'd seen arena-sized crowds swaying to a particular song or pumped up for the big radio tune, but this was more like something you'd see on the Discovery Channel—a wild dance ceremony in some far-off torchlit corner of the world, drums beating frenetically.

It's the diehards at Phish shows who seem to most enjoy these frenzied moments, who seem to really have a moving experience. Skinny as can be, like they've been stranded on a desert island for years, and they find, somewhere, a ferocious energy. They dance *hard*, with everything they've got, for the entire set, cooling down a bit for the slower numbers but still working it. They drink a lot of water, smoke a few joints in the dark—both the water jug and the joint get passed down the row—and then between sets they sit down on the lawn, unwind a bit. The first set usually lasts about an hour and twenty minutes. Do you know what it's like to dance for eighty minutes straight? At some point in the set I always have to sit down for a moment. I usually get a cramp or simply run out of gas. And I'm in pretty good shape. I think these tourheads have a reserve tank to draw from, which they tap into when the lights go down and Phish takes the stage. In the tank sloshes a powerful cocktail of adrenaline and drugs, and the music is like a zap of lightning that kicks them into gear. It reminds me of that scene in the old Frankenstein movie where the zombie monster lies on the table, pale and lifeless, and then lightning strikes and the monster opens his eyes and he's instantly ready to go. The music is a bolt of life for Phishheads.

Have you ever run down a street at night with alcohol buzzing through your veins? You feel like the fastest guy on the planet, like you could jump over a building. Except it doesn't last long and you come down after a few minutes, gasping for air. Well,

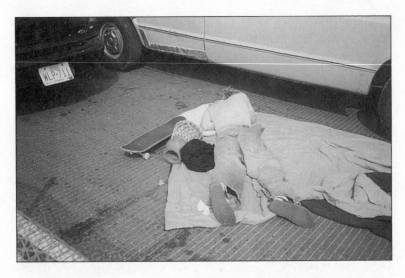

imagine being able to keep up that sort of energy for an hour or
so—that's what it's like at a Phish show. I have a friend who
never runs anywhere except when he's drunk, in which case he
tears about—dives into bushes, climbs trees, hurdles fences.
Sober, he doesn't even walk very fast, and running, I mean, forget
it. He *hates* to run. But with alcohol racing around inside his
body, he's able to tap this well of energy and just take off. I think
some Phishheads are able to fuel their tank in the same way—
they transform into super-energized versions of their normal
selves.

Because for them this is what it's all about. This is what it all
comes down to on tour: the show. You have to Get It Up for the
show. No matter how far you've traveled, no matter how worn
out you feel, no matter how little money you have in your
pocket . . . who cares? You're here and your band is taking the
stage. That's why diehard tourheads enjoy the moment even
more—this is it for them, the big payoff. What else is there to
look forward to? Tomorrow means another traffic jam, more rest
areas, a scramble for a decent meal. The end of the tour means
finding another job, since you quit the last one.

We tend to think of dropouts as delinquents, avoiders, cowards. But the thing we don't realize is that dropping out isn't easy. Oddly enough, it takes a certain perseverance. Anybody in America can find a job. Anybody can find an apartment and a shower and a roof over his head. In a way it takes a certain willfulness *not* to have these things. Life is much easier with a steady job and an apartment. Life on the road, riding the highways each day, takes a scrappiness that most of us don't have. We need the security of nine-to-five with benefits and ten vacation days per year and Sunday afternoons in the park. It would be hard to come up with a figure for how many Phishheads really are on tour for years, who truly are dropouts. At least a couple thousand. And add to that many, many more thousands who go to maybe four or five shows per tour—an adventure in itself.

Phish is tapping a nerve in America. It's the same nerve the Dead found, but with a different generation. It's hard to define the nerve, exactly. It's a lot of things rolled into one. Somehow our culture is not offering up everything that young people need, that young people search for. What's missing in our youth culture of video games and satellite dishes and the World Wide Web? What's missing in a country in which the fastest-growing sport is golf? Adventure. Adventure is partly what's missing. The Phish tour promises adventure. But it's more than that. We don't really have any ritualized celebrations in America. The holidays, yeah, but the holidays mean football games on Thanksgiving and the malls at Christmas. We don't have any rituals. We don't celebrate the coming of the spring. We don't celebrate the harvest moon. When was the last time you celebrated anything? I mean, when was the last time you let your hair down and howled at the moon on a clear autumn night? Humans have been doing this sort of thing for centuries, as a way to celebrate life, the joy of it.

Phish shows are becoming an American ritual. People turn out year after year to hear the same band play the same songs at the same time of year. And it is precisely this continuity, the ritual of it, that in a way brings a magic to the show, makes the fan feel like he is part of the event. The shows provide a timeline, a kind of calendar to divide up the year. In America, our rituals are sports and television—going to the ball park or sitting in front of the tube. These are anemic rituals, without any real bite or celebration, and they don't really deserve to be called rituals anyway. The American Dream at the millennium is television and the Internet—how much time you get to watch the tube or surf the net. And if you're really lucky, if you've really made it, then the American Dream means getting to play a lot of golf.

At night, after the show, the campgrounds come alive. Outside the amphitheaters and hockey arenas, people beat drums and dance in circles. Wherever Phish goes, the sound of drums can be heard—drums beating in parking lots, drums at night, drums in the sunshine. It provides a weirdly atavistic background to the whole thing. People truly do howl into the night.

If one person in every family learned to the play the drums and once a week you gathered outside and hopped around for a few hours, we'd all be much happier. I'm not kidding around here. I mean it. Get a bongo drum, go to your backyard or your neighborhood park or the beach, bring a bunch of friends, build a bonfire, bring a flask of wine, and have someone start hammering away on the bongo. I dare you to stay still. I dare you not to dance until you drop. You wouldn't believe the release.

Americans work harder than anyone else in the world. That's a fact. According to a *New York Times* report, we work 350 more hours per year than Europeans (that equals nine work weeks) and 70 more hours per year than the Japanese. We have the strongest economy in the world, but also the busiest work force. No one has any time. Who do you know who works forty hours a week anymore? Humans weren't meant to sit in offices all day. We didn't evolve to hunch over a computer, butts glued to a chair.

May Day is the kind of celebration we need in America. May Day began as a Roman holiday in honor of Flora, goddess of flowers and spring. The festival celebrated the new spring and fertility and just nature itself. The holiday spread across Europe and became a tradition in England, where for a while it was banned due to general decadence. You can still find towns in Britain today that celebrate by dancing around the Maypole. In Turkey, May Day is a national holiday. In parts of Eastern Europe, May Day was a Socialist holiday.

Nathaniel Hawthorne wrote a short story called "The Maypole of Merry Mount" about an early American colony with a maypole at the forest's edge. With the Indians, the settlers wore masks of goat and bear, fixed horns on their heads, drank wine and danced around the maypole—a slender pine tree decked with garlands.

"On the Eve of St. John," Hawthorne wrote, "they felled whole acres of the forest to make bonfires, and danced by the blaze all night, crowned with garlands, and throwing flowers into the flame. . . . Its votaries danced round it, once, at least, in every month; sometimes they called it their religion, or their altar; but always, it was the banner staff of Merry Mount."

It was a pretty wild scene for seventeenth-century America— too wild for the neighboring Puritans ("most dismal wretches," according to Hawthorne), who eventually tore down the maypole and punished the revelers. Hawthorne's story is based on fact. There was a settlement in Massachusetts near present-day Quincy called Mount Wollaston, or "Merry Mount." In 1625, Thomas Morton established a trading post in the area, put up a maypole, and invited the Indians—whom he found to be more "full of humanity" than the English—to dance with the colonists. The festivities angered and upset Governor John Endicott, who ordered the maypole chopped down. Morton wound up in trouble for dealing firearms to the Indians and fled to England.

So the maypole celebrations, the welcoming of spring with attendant rites and partying, never got more than a toehold in America, and it was quickly stomped out. I'm not suggesting that Phish shows are a modern-day Merry Mount. After all, there isn't any clear connection to spring or fertility or any of that stuff. But the music, the dancing, the celebration outdoors, the strange costumes, the ritual of it all—all this is there. Phish shows are probably the closest we get to Merry Mount.

In college we had this party called Bavaria each spring. A pig roast and a parade. A few of us dressed up in what we imagined to be Bavarian style—knee-high socks, shorts, and suspenders. One year someone even hauled in a sheep for the party, which just stood there silent and still until someone poked it with a stick. None of us knew a thing about Bavaria, and it was really just an excuse to have a party. But we put on a parade. Now this was something to see. Trombones and trumpets and we all trooped wildly around campus, beating homemade drums (mine was a tin garbage can) and singing this song over and over: "I love a parade, love a parade, love a parade. . . ." Then we'd come back and drink more beer and dance by the fire with a chunk of pig in hand. It was different from our normal routine of standing beside a basement keg guzzling watery beer in plastic cups. Here we were, hundreds of us, dancing around in the springtime with the drums beating and the music and everything blooming and the pig cooking. It really was connected to the spring and being out-doors and being young. And it wasn't about the Internet or the movies or museums or books. It was a real in-the-flesh celebration. In a strange way, it became a ritual. I'm not sure why I'm writing about this now. I haven't thought of Bavaria in a while. But somehow talking about Merry Mount brought back Bavaria, and now I'm feeling depressed with my Bavaria days behind me.

My brother has joined me for this leg of the tour. His name is Brendan, but he's known to everyone as Skins (too hard to explain). He just graduated from Harvard and is not sure what he's going to do career-wise. He plans on heading out to Colorado in the winter with a few friends, maybe wait tables . . . the fear of every parent: send him to Harvard and he ends up in Aspen a ski bum. The Phish tour should be perfect.

He's the one who introduced me to Phish in the first place and we've been to a bunch of shows together. Also, Skins has seen a number of the big acts in recent years—the Rolling Stones, U2, Dave Matthews—so he knows what else is out there in terms of live rock and roll and he thinks that no one comes close to Phish.

For Skins it all started with Guns N' Roses. It was a birthday present from my dad: two tickets to GNR at Madison Square Garden on a school night. My dad thought it would be fine. You know, the two of them going off to a rock and roll concert together, riding the train into the city. He brought a book along for the slow parts of the night. Well, things started off with the strippers on stage and it progressed from there. . . . But my dad was okay with it all. Surprised, I think, by the level of decadence and probably very unimpressed with the music itself. But what really bothered him was something else entirely: the cigarette lighters. People flicked on their lighters for the one or two slow songs and waved them above their heads. My dad had never seen *this* before. Never heard of such a thing. At the time he was a prep school headmaster, and things like fire hazards were very much on his mind. He asked security if they would do something about this, which I'm sure the security guy thought, *What . . .* ?

A few days after the show my dad wrote a letter on his headmaster's stationery to the fire chief of New York City, expressing his concern, and believe it or not he did get a reply from the fire department, saying they'd look into the matter.

Where the hell am I going with this? Not sure. Who's to say there has to be a solid story line always moving forward? You're bound to get distracted here and there. It's like being on tour— you never get to the next venue without diversions. Anyway, we're in New Jersey for the next two days. I'm not sure I've mentioned this yet. Phish plays Friday and Saturday night at the PNC Bank Arts Center (formerly known as the Garden State Arts Center, a much more dignified name—though admittedly it's not as bad as what happened with Great Woods, rechristened the Tweeter Center, a name I refuse to acknowledge and am embarrassed to see now on my screen). The PNC Bank Arts Center is like all the other venues—open-air, amphitheater-shaped, with a roof covering the front section and a wide swath of general-admission lawn in the back. It's in Holmdel, New Jersey, not far from the shore. In fact, our motel is right on a boardwalky stretch of the Jersey shore, which I'll get to later.

The big news around here today is Bruce Springsteen and the E Street Band kicking off a fifteen-night run tonight at New Jersey's Continental Airlines Arena. Fifteen nights all at the same place, each one sold out. Bruce is of course a Jersey boy, and this is the big reunion tour after ten years apart from the E Street Band. The local papers are full of Bruce. He's a hero in this part of the world.

At the show, two noteworthy things occur:

The first is a guy in a Hawaiian shirt (unbuttoned) and a captain's hat (white with ropy yellow trim) running up and down the aisle shouting, "Bruuuuuce! Bruuuuuce!" He's red-eyed and pot-bellied and drunk. It's a safe bet he's a Jersey boy. He starts his routine before Phish takes the stage. The strange thing is, he gets no response from the crowd, even when he turns around to face them, cheerleader-fashion. No one so much as lifts a finger to support his call for Bruce. I guess it's not surprising, really. Most Phishheads could probably care less about Bruce Springsteen. Any time you walk by a VW bus in the parking lot the only thing you hear is Phish—maybe some Dead or Bob Marley, but that's about it. Our Hawaiian man doesn't tire easily, nor does he show a shred of embarrassment as he keeps up the routine full-bore until the house lights go out.

The second noteworthy thing happens when a fan jumps on stage. He has a few seconds in the spotlight before the Yellow Shirts come to take him away. Up there in the bright lights he doesn't know what to do or where to go, so after leaping on stage he stands still for a moment. I don't think he imagined he would have much time to kill after making the big leap. He considers for a second walking in Trey's direction, thinks better of it. He looks all of a sudden profoundly embarrassed. At least if he were a girl he could run up and throw his arms around Trey and everything would be fine. But he's not. He looks like an average suburban kid caught in a very awkward situation, about to maybe stick his hands in his pockets and stare down at his feet. But at the last second he saves himself by turning towards the audience and throwing his arms in the air in a gesture of total triumph. At which point the Yellow Shirts close in. The timing is perfect and he's able to exit with both hands in the air, a face-saving way to go down.

I try to see where security carts him off to. For a moment I consider trailing them for a bit of investigative journalism. But I don't want to get into some weird chase scene around the PNC Bank Arts Center.

98 Degrees

July 16, The Jersey Shore

Tough start to the day for Skins. Each morning he takes out a green elastic cord, loops it around a doorknob, and pulls on it slowly for about ten minutes to strengthen his shoulder, which he separated in a snowboarding accident six months ago. So there he was, standing in his boxer shorts by the bathroom door, working out, with his head turned around because *Police Academy 5* was on HBO. I should say that this cord is made of a strong elastic fiber and it takes a fair amount of strength to perform these exercises. You really have to pull hard. It should also be mentioned that the Fountain Motel's doorknob was perhaps too small and rickety for the job. And finally I should note that my brother is a big fan of the *Police Academy* series, and was therefore not paying enough attention to his exercises.

In the middle of the routine, the cord slipped from the doorknob and with a wicked snap ricocheted straight into his groin. My brother screamed as loud as I've ever heard him scream, ran across the room, and launched onto the bed.

"Get in the fetal position," I said. "Curl up."

"UUUUUUUHHHHHHHH!!!!" He was all teeth and gums.

"Stay just like that."

So now it's an hour later and we're at a diner on the Jersey shore for a midday breakfast. Skins still looks a little woozy. He's not eating much, barely talking, pupils still dilated. We're listening to the conversation from the next booth, a breakfast meeting between a down-on-their-luck rock band and some kind of industry talent-scout type. I scribble down what he's saying on a bus schedule.

"I like what you guys did last night with that song, where it was going, but then you came in with that Stones riff and it was too much of a ripoff. You gotta be less obvious. We need something that can be sold to the industry. Any one of those songs that you've brought to the table can be reworked. Mix and match, see what makes it work. Like with what's-it-called—'Pain and Suffering'—or 'Let it Go', they can be worked on. People want to sing along to this shit. They're over the angry. They're my age and they're over the angry. I think we need to go back to the drawing board. Let's go back and think about what the real talents of the band are. It's about making the stuff better. Don't get emotional. You guys gotta give this some thought. I'm not going to let you guys go. I know your talent, but I want to be more involved."

The whole time Talent Scout is talking, the bandmates mumble a few words here and there and poke at their eggs. But they pretty much let the guy hold forth. Clearly, they don't have other record people knocking down their door or else they wouldn't sit here for this, smoking cigarettes, drinking coffee, red-eyed from last night, closing in on thirty. Talent Scout has touched a nerve, though. These guys are frustrated. They hardly look at him.

"You guys could definitely work on some things. Like with the vocals, man. With the vocals, man, you gotta be right on. *Right* on. They're following your lead. The vocals could be tighter and better. But you guys got to give this some thought, if this is where you want to go, if this is where you want to be. We need something for the industry. That's the reality of it."

"No! Being an artist has *nothing* to do with the reality of the industry." Finally the lead singer has had enough. "We're *not* going to think about it. We're just going to play."

"You have to think about it or this whole meeting is pointless," Talent Scout says. "That's the reality of the industry."

"We gotta do what we like," the singer says. "It's as simple as that." He wears a white t-shirt. His hair is still wet from his early-afternoon shower.

"Hey, you can still do your own thing," Talent Scout says. "I'm not saying that. Come on, this shouldn't be an artist-versus-the-industry thing. You don't have to be, you know, Sheryl Crow Meets the Counting Crows. I'm not saying that. But you really need to ask some questions. Where are we going? Where do we want to be?"

"It's not like that," the singer says. But he sounds defeated. Drinks some more coffee. Stares into his plate. Smokes another cigarette.

We head back to the motel for some rest. Skins is still a bit out of it. The pain's gone, but he seems dazed. The Fountain Motel is right on the beach. It's a total dump, beside a closed-down nightclub and across from an arcade with outdated video games. The nightclub's marquee reads, crookedly, LADIES NIGHT. The windows are broken. A few old men sit on benches along the boardwalk. The town, about a mile away, isn't much better. The sun beats down on you every step. No shade anywhere except inside shops and delis, which are empty. Photographs of Bruce Springsteen as a young man in just about every place you go. No photos for sale, and no glossy professional shots. Mostly black-and-white pictures of a sweaty Bruce on stage in a small bar, or a sweaty Bruce after a show with a heavyset bartender, smiling for the camera. This really is Bruce Country. Asbury Park is a few miles down the road. I can picture him here twenty-five years ago, setting up for the night at a small club along the boardwalk, looking out the window at the beach and wondering who's going to show up tonight.

The beach itself is enormous, a long walk from the sandy boardwalk to the water. A midsummer haze hangs over the ocean and a few planes cut back and forth, dragging along banners. Not many people on the beach. Clusters of napping Phishheads, quite

pale, interspersed among gum-snapping Jersey girls. A big mus-
cleman parades by in a tiny bathing suit. Skins and I plop down
in the sand without towels. The Fountain Motel's towels are
threadbare and too small—post-shower you can't even wrap one
around your waist without being totally exposed. The Phishheads a few yards away from us don't have towels, either. They
are fast asleep, so an interview is out of the question. In fact, they
haven't moved an inch since we've been here, lying flat on their
bellies, covered in tie-dyes. Two nights in a row at the same
venue presents an interesting challenge on tour: what do you do
the second day? There's nowhere to travel, no venue three hundred miles away to get to before seven p.m. Chasing Phish
imposes a kind of order on your life. It demands a plan even if
you don't feel like it. Tired, hung over, worn out, it doesn't matter. You get on the road, look at the map, and drive. You get gas,
check your mileage, wash the bugs off the window while filling
up. This is your job. When you take away the road for a day, you
take away the one shred of order to the tour. Without the seven
p.m. deadline, a sluggishness sets in. Too much down time. Too
much time to think. Part of the appeal of the road is that you
really don't have time alone to think. No time for self-reflection.
You're in a cramped car on a mission and there's no time to
examine anything too closely.

"Are you up for a swim?" I say to Skins.

"Sure."

"How you feeling with, you know . . . ?"

"Better. I'm worried about the waves."

Things improve by the evening. Somehow our passes have
been upgraded from aftershow to all access, which means
tonight we can go anywhere. There's a whole series of different
passes, each with a certain level of access. People with passes are
always glancing at one another's passes. It's a way of sizing each
other up, determining rank. How well do *you* know the band?

NUBAR ALEXANIAN

We head directly for the stage. With ALL ACCESS stuck on your t-shirt you really are a star. The security guys keep their arms folded on their chest and nod slightly when you twist to present the pass. We walk up a ramp and onto the stage. Phish is about halfway through the first set, in the middle of a long jam. The stage lights are everywhere, spinning wildly. Usually the light guy is right on the money. He knows all the songs by heart and times his light show with the music's transitions. But every so often Phish wanders off, musically, and the light guy—and everyone else—has no idea what's going on. This is one of those times. Skins and I stand just outside the circle of light, in the side-stage darkness. Great view of the band. Trey's expression during a long jam is odd. He scrunches his face, baring a lot of teeth. When you stub your toe and there's that second or two before the pain comes . . . that's what Trey looks like right now. A bit like Bill Gates, actually—a shaggier version. Beside Trey is Mike with his big hair, head bent over his bass. Page swivels between four keyboards, all within an arm's length. He wears black leather shoes and a collared shirt, by far the best-dressed in the band. Behind them Fishman plays the drums in a dress. He looks grumpy. Every fan in the front row looks starry-eyed and high.

Not much behind-the-scenes activity up here on stage. Not much work for the road crew during the show itself. They work like mad before and after, but now they sit on boxes and relax. No one dances. I'd say there are maybe twenty people on stage. Fifteen or so are clearly on the payroll, then a few people who also scored all access and who, like us, stand around trying to blend in. The crew doesn't pay attention to the music. Some of them even nap, finding lounge space between boxes. It's actually not that loud on stage. The speakers project out to the crowd, so on stage the music isn't nearly as clear. Fuzzy, almost.

Behind a tall black curtain, down a walkway, double doors swing open every couple minutes to some sort of deeper backstage area.

"Why don't we go see what's down there?" Skins says.

"Maybe later."

"It could be interesting."

"I'm going to stay here. You can go."

"Come on, let's check it out," he says. "We've got the passes."

"I don't know. It just feels weird. I think we should stay here. It's a good view and all." I don't want to move. I don't want to run into trouble with security, but that's not it really. I'm afraid of suddenly being cast into the spotlight. Like as soon as we leave this dark little corner one of the roaming lights will nab me and then thirty thousand fans will see me here on stage, frozen, mouth open, staring straight into the lights, and I won't be able to move. I have a similar problem with heights. When I'm up there I completely freeze, as if any movement will upset the balance of things.

"Look," Skins says, "I'm going to check it out."

"Fine."

He walks behind the curtain.

After a moment I follow him. We pick our way around the back of the stage, careful not to step on any wires. Big arrows taped to the floor mark paths around the stage. (A few years ago, before a show, Trey fell through a hole in the stage, sprained his ankle badly, and since then the crew has made sure to mark paths clearly.) The swinging doors lead to a small cafeteria. Three beefy guys with long beards and tattoos sit at a table, and when we come in they look up.

We stop just inside the door.

"The, ah, cafeteria," I say to Skins.

"Yeah. That's right."

We turn back to reclaim our sidestage post. As the first set ends, the band walks single-file across the stage, towards a white door guarded by security. They walk right past us, and for a million dollars I wouldn't say a word to any of them right now. They seem, I don't know, like from another world, completely untouchable. It's weird, because I've seen these guys around Burlington plenty of times—Page on the squash court, Trey on a ski slope, Gordon at a bar—and it truly isn't a big deal. Just the guys in Phish. But here on stage, walking past us, with the crowd in a frenzy, they seem almost unreal.

They disappear behind the white door and I crane my neck around to peer after them, which makes the security woman sitting on a stool by the door suspicious of me. She glances at my pass and shakes her head. She shouldn't worry. There's no way I'd go down there even if I could.

There must be a pass higher than all access.

This is the second time Skins has been backstage this summer. He doesn't like to admit it, but a few weeks ago he ended up backstage at a 98 Degrees concert. 98 Degrees, if you don't know, is one of the hot "boy bands" this summer (the other hot ones being the Backstreet Boys and 'N SYNC). Five or six guys dress up in matching outfits and sing pop songs to screaming teenage girls while dancing choreographed routines that involve clapping their hands, tipping their caps, leapfrogging one another, the whole deal. It's pretty embarrassing. Skins has this detailed defense about how the only reason he went was because his friend is dating this woman, Tatyana Ali, who was opening up for 98 Degrees, and that he himself didn't have *any* interest at all in seeing 98 Degrees, let alone hanging around backstage with them.* It turned out, however, that the concert wasn't just 98 Degrees and Tatyana Ali. There was a whole lineup of acts, part of the Nickelodeon "All That" concert series.

I asked Skins what that backstage scene was like compared to Phish.

"There was a lot of people back there, since there were five or six different musical acts performing. A lot more people and a lot more music-industry types. Back in that eating area at Phish it looked like a bunch of crew—longhaired, overweight, meaty guys. This was more crew mixed in within second-rate acts combing their hair. We met a bunch of Tatyana's dancers, who were all dressed the same and were pretty attractive. It was a very chaotic scene. At Phish everyone was kind of hanging out, watching the show, drinking beer, sitting on the props. Here, everyone was doing something. Dancers were running back and forth into this coed changing room."

Skins and company did their best to ignore the actual concert and just think about the party back at the hotel, which was starting to look pretty good if all these dancers were going to be there. But first they had a show to get through.

"There was one terrible boy band that went on first," Skins said. "Their name was No Authority. I remember that because as we walked out of the concert we were given tapes of No Authority. We were given little singles tapes. Only it wasn't singles, it was snippets. One of their lines was, *Hit me with your seven digits*. We sort of thought that the fan demographic would be like thirteen-year-old girls, fourteen-year-old girls. It turns out they were pretty much eight-, nine-year-old girls. The oldest girl there,

---

*A little background. Skins's Harvard classmate George is the one dating Tatyana Ali, famous from her role on the television show *The Fresh Prince of Bel-Air* and who is also a Harvard freshman. "Everybody knew who she was," Skins said. "George swooped in and snatched her up in the first few weeks of school." Which got him the nickname Hollywood George. George promised Skins & Company a backstage party deal with Tatyana's dancers, a major reason why they made the trip.

I mean the *oldest* girl there, was probably fourteen. And that was rare, to see a fourteen-year-old. It was basically all these girls and their parents driving down in their minivans, and the door would open up and all these eight- and nine-year-old girls would pile out, screaming in anticipation.

"In between acts they would play songs over the speakers and they had a DJ who was getting the crowd worked up, and the girls were just going crazy screaming, thousands of girls screaming."

"What did that sound like?" I said.

"High-pitched. A little more dissonant and harsh on the ears. And then the DJ played the Backstreet Boys ballad and there were probably five, six thousand girls singing in unison along with the Backstreet Boys. It was pretty clear that, you know, as much as they liked 98 Degrees, it was clear where their loyalties lay. And I don't think the eight-to-nine-year-old girls care that much that 98 Degrees is way more jacked than the Backstreet Boys."*

Backstage, things weren't so bad. They got to hang out in Tatyana's dressing room, where they could check out the dancers at close range, who apparently were shedding one spandexed ensemble after another between songs and never closed the door. And they even met Will Smith's producer, which on the back-stage Nickelodeon food chain is at the very top of the pyramid.

But then everything started to go wrong. Hollywood George talked about having to get back on the bus, and thanks guys for coming. Skins and company didn't know what to do. It was awkward to bring it up: "Uh, George . . . about the hotel scene . . .

---

*The matching outfits for 98 Degrees tend towards tank tops and unzipped vests to show off their muscles, which are in fact pretty big and make the Backstreet Boys truly seem like little scrawny kids romping around in extra-large t-shirts. When they perform (I've seen it on MTV), each guy in 98 Degrees is in a state of constant flex, like a bodybuilder posing for a panel of judges—only these guys have to sing and dance through the grimace of flexing, which seems especially disturbing when you consider the eight-to-nine-year-old demographic at the Nickelodeon "All That" event.

remember how we were, you know, supposed to be a part of that?" There they were, escorted backstage by Hollywood George, putting in their time at this Nickelodeon scene but for the promise of hotel rooms and spandex and whatever else. Hollywood George ditched them. Left them hanging, left them to walk back across the parking lot, past the minivans playing snippets from the giveaway No Authority tape.

The difference between a 98 Degrees show and a Phish show is sort of like the difference between a lecture where the speaker stands at the podium reading from a prepared speech and one where he stands up and talks directly to the audience, never looking down at a sheet in front of him. The prepared speech can be fine sometimes, but it's never great, and in fact it's often boring and quite annoying to have someone up there just reading to you. Insulting even. The guy up there winging it, on the other hand, may fall flat on his face. He might make a fool of himself. But he also might absolutely nail it—connect with the audience the way a prepared talk could never connect with people. Because it's a working brain, a man thinking in front of you, and that can be very exciting. When Phish takes the stage there is no script. You don't know what you're going to get. And of course they're not always on. But there they are right in front of you figuring it out.

A couple of days ago, in the *Boston Globe*, Jon Fishman said, "You can come see us one night, and we're an entirely different band from the night before. It's not something that we've done intentionally to keep people on tour. I could not imagine going out on tour and playing the same every night."

Camp Oswego

July 17–18, Oswego County Airport, New York

A narrow road snakes through farm country towards Oswego, just north of Syracuse. Nothing at all around here. Trees. Barns. A few gas stations. It's seven-thirty p.m. and this single-lane road is backed up for miles, jammed with carloads of fans waiting to pass through the gate to Oswego County Airport, the sight of the midtour weekend-long bash. Since Kansas, people have been talking about Oswego, the biggest party of the summer. With no motels around, camping at the airport is the only option for sixty thousand people. That's part of the point this weekend—everyone gets together for two days and nights, the whole tour in a few square miles of runway. At the last gas station, I spotted the nitrous team from Camden, the earpiece group. I bet they have big plans for Oswego.

We roll forward a few feet.

By ten p.m. we've inched along maybe a half-mile. This is ridiculous. We've missed half the show already. I can hear the music now and then, drifting across the fields. This whole thing is stupid. A waste of time. *Oswego?* What the hell am I doing here in goddamn Oswego? No band is worth this.

Oswego locals sit on front porches and watch us. Strange people, they're probably thinking. Stupid people to come all this way and sit in traffic. . . . And they're right. I want out right now. I'm sick of it all. Couldn't the band have organized this better? They knew all these people would be showing up here on this narrow stretch of backroad with flies buzzing around.

In front of us, a few feet from the Jimmy, a guy leans on his van, looking up at the sky. His dreadlocks are gathered together, wrapped in a band, and point straight off his forehead in unicorn fashion.

"I'm a philosopher," he says to a skateboarder standing beside him. He says it seriously. Not a shred of humor. The skateboarder nods.

"Did you hear that?" I say to Skins. "A philosopher? Are you *kidding* me? Look at him. I've got to write that down. Philosopher! 'I'm a philosopher.' I can't *believe* this fucking guy. Who does he think . . . You got a pen? This is good stuff. I want to write this down."

"Your eavesdropping-to-interviewing ratio is skyrocketing," Skins says, handing me a pen.

"Yeah, well . . . Hold on a sec, let me get this down."

"I think you should do some more interviews."

"I have already."

"Not enough," he says. "I just think for the book you need to go and talk to people and find out what they're doing, where they're from. You could get some good stuff. I don't know . . . I think it's got to be more than just your observations."

"Well, I like doing it my way. And you could help, you know. Like why don't you step out and interview those two over there?"

"The guys with the Metallica t-shirts? Nice try."

He's right. I wouldn't interview them either. Tattoos. Baggy pants. Nose rings. The thick kind of nose rings, you know—the ones that loop through both nostrils. These two Metallica dudes are probably seventeen or eighteen years old and clearly not Phish fans. In the last few hours, I've seen dozens of teenagers like these two who seem to be up to no good, who seem to be here for the drug scene, not the music. My guess is they don't plan to go into the show. One pack of kids has passed by a few times now. Five of them with nose rings and shaved heads and backwards baseball hats. They circle the idling cars like a pack of wolves, staring down everyone they pass. They appear to be on the look-out for something. Who knows what. Girls? Drugs?

A car of longhairs behind us pays no attention to the roaming kids. They crank up the music and dance on the street. Meat Loaf blasts from their van . . . *Baby baby let me sleep on it* . . . A woman with long braids and a purple t-shirt and flowery skirt stretches her arms out like an airplane's wings and swoops around the van.

We arrive at the gate about midnight. By now people are screaming out their windows, dancing on hoods, running around like madmen, skateboarding over broken glass. One skinny dude zips by on a motorized scooter with tiny wheels. He's standing up on the thing, dodging people and cars, and his laugh, my God, it's spooky.

The air is thick with pot. I walk over to the box office to pick up our tickets for the weekend. A guy in his thirties hops out of his car and heads in my direction.

"Do you play paintball?" he says.

"*What?*" The last thing I need at this point is some whacked-out bearded guy selling drugs.

"Paintball."

"I don't know what you're talking about."

"Paintball," he says again, staring straight at me, wide-eyed. "You know, with the guns. My brother's got these fields in New Jersey, man. Two of them. Two open fields. Are you into it?"

"Well, I don't—"

"It's crazy, man. People get into it. Real into it. They hide in trees, man, and dress up in camo. You get some guys who are in it real serious. You should come down if you're interested. Check it out, you know."

I'm not sure why this dude is talking to me at all, let alone about his brother's paintball fields in New Jersey for a bunch of sickos in camouflage. What the fuck is going on here? What's wrong with this place? I just want to pass through the gate, find a camping spot, and forget about tonight.

He keeps talking, the paintball guy. He seems a bit wired. His eyes dart around in their sockets and he keeps glancing over his shoulder for someone in the dark. I think he said his wife, but maybe not. Then he tells me he's here at Oswego to interview for a job with the road crew. Tonight. Tonight's the interview, he says, and he just got here from New Jersey, down by the shore area, and do I know someone or other named Jim who he's supposed to meet between sets for this interview to work the rest of the summer tour? He's not sure where to meet exactly, just to ask for Jim.

When he looks over his shoulder again I take off.

I hurry back to the Jimmy with the tickets in hand. A girl standing outside of a van stares at me strangely. She's out of it, I can tell in a glance. Two of her friends stand behind her and also watch me.

Keep your eyes down, you're almost there. . . . I've got one leg in the Jimmy when she calls out, "Hey . . . can you help us out?" She speaks slowly, like a character in a dream.

"Actually, we're in kind of a hurry," I say.

"Hey." She looks back at her friends and then refocuses on me. "Hey . . . do you have . . . tickets?"

"Yeah, we don't need any."

"Two . . . tickets?"

"Yeah, two tickets. Listen—"

"Is . . . is that your brother?"

It's like talking to a ghost. I don't think there are bones or body underneath her baggy dress.

"What does she want?" Skins whispers from the passenger seat.

"I don't know. Let's go." I close the door.

"Hey," she calls out again. "Hey . . . could you drive our van in . . . with your ticket . . . and we'll hide . . . in the back?"

"Ah, I don't think that would be smart."

"We'll hide in the back and you could drive it . . . with your ticket." She looks back at her friends again, who appear in the dark to be gently swaying, like plants.

"Didn't you see those signs on the road coming in?" I say.

"Which signs?"

"The ones all over the place that said they check inside vehicles for people trying to sneak in."

"I heard they . . . weren't checking."

"Well, they are. I'm not going to do it. Sorry."

As I turn the ignition, I catch her eye for a moment and her face has completely changed. For a split second the spaced-out zombie is gone, replaced by a nasty witch. Scary. She hates me for not helping her out, for being one of those types who pay attention to rules and abide by security regulations. She hates me for not joining in the tour spirit. I get this same look of disgust whenever I ask for my seat inside a show. Someone is *always* in my seat. There's this unwritten rule that you should be able to wander wherever you want at a show, and if you take someone's seat, then that person has no right to ask for it, and if that person does in fact ask for it, then he is a schmuck.

We drive through the gate. No turning back. We won't leave this place for two days. We follow the line of cars down the airport runway. Tents and cars and vans as far as you can see, a city sprung from the airport.

Each of the last three years, Phish has hosted a big summer blowout on deserted airstrips in the Northeast. They build a stage at one end of the runway, wall off an area for the concert, and then everyone camps along the miles and miles of leftover airfield. It's a weird idea, but it makes sense for a lot of reasons. First of all, these airports are in the middle of nowhere, so you don't have the hassle of dealing with a city. The runways themselves provide adequate avenues for all the trucks and trailers hauling necessary supplies. And there seems to be a number of these decaying airports around. At the end of the cold war, many U.S. Air Force bases closed down and are now financially depressed areas, hungry for any kind of business. So Phish comes in with forkloads of money and says, in effect, Let us have your airport for the weekend. I'm not sure what the story is with the Oswego airport—it looks kind of small-time—but last year the

big air-base show was in northern Maine, way at the top of the
state in potato-farming country. Loring Air Force Base was the
sight—a spooky, barbed-wired place dotted with giant hangars
on the horizon that once housed B-52 bombers. Seventy thousand Phishheads showed up for the Loring weekend last summer.
Phish called it "Lemonwheel," and it was the biggest concert
event of the year in North America.

They are expecting a similar crowd here at Oswego. Every inch
of camping space along the runway seems to be taken already.
Guys with flares wave us on, away from the grass, to a parking
area away from the campsite. I swerve out of line and tear across
the runway towards the grass. I get out quickly and pop open the
back. "Come on," I say to Skins, expecting a flare to chase after us.
"Let's claim a camping spot before they're all gone."

A tall guy leaning on a jeep beside us looks over and says,
"That's what I like to see, baby, another Chevy Blazer. Check it
out. We're the Blazer Brothers. All right. That's what I'm talking
about. All right. I love traveling in the Blazer, man, sleepin' in the
back with the seat down. Riding in style. Hey, I'm Mike G and
over there, that's Chester. How ya'll doing?"

"Pretty good."

"All right. You guys need anything, let me know." Rap music blasts from Mike G's car and he dances in place while talking to us. "I got it all, man. Any pharmaceutical you need. Black Beauties, Xanax. I got some L2 that will get you spun. Whatever you need. I even got some toilet paper, you know what I'm saying. If you forgot it, just ask whenever. No problem, you're in the neighborhood."

"Thanks."

"And you like jazz? I got it all. You into jazz? We'll get some jazz going on Sunday morning. Some Coltrane, know what I'm saying? Yeah. We'll smoke up on me and just chill all day. All right. You're in the neighborhood. It's cool."

Mike G's traveling companion, Chester, dances by himself a few feet away, paying no attention to us or to anything, really. Chester is short and squat and spins slowly around in a circle, on beat, a cigarette hanging from his mouth. I think he's flying on some Mike G pharmaceuticals.

Mike G gives me the tour of his Blazer's stereo system. He's limby and narrow and can't stay still. He bounces in place and knows all the words to his rap music by heart. He raps while he talks. "So these speakers are phat . . . *out on the street with my posse* . . . take a look, go ahead. And then when people want to go to sleep we take the party on the road with this baby." Mike G hauls out a giant oval-shaped boom box with speakers all over it. "Me and Chester hit the road, you know, when it gets real late. Keep the party going."

Still spinning, Chester doesn't know any of the words, although once in a while he'll get a verse . . . *the bitches, the bitches* . . . His eyes are barely open, a sliver of white. I can't imagine him talking.

Skins and I sit on the back of the Jimmy drinking beer. In the next few minutes dozens of people try to sell us drugs. So far, just sitting here, we've been offered nuggets (pot), shrooms (mushrooms), tabs (acid), liquid (another form of acid), and X (Ecstasy).

It's out of control. Not a cop in sight, and the dealers aren't even whispering. They come right up and meet you square in the eye. Usually, dealers are a bit more subtle. You can spot them pretty easily. They always travel alone, almost exclusively male, and they walk against the grain, meaning they walk through a crowd headed in the opposite direction, whispering their drug as they go. But here at Oswego it's a free-for-all. Everyone's selling. With no chance of getting nabbed by a cop, no strategy necessary. Just step right up.

I talked to one one dealer and said I wouldn't use his name. He said acid is the best moneymaker on tour by far. "It's so easy," he said. "So easy. You buy a sheet for one hundred twenty bucks, a single hit sells for five bucks—that's five hundred dollars. That's how I financed my trip last summer. It paid for my gas, my cigarettes, my food. It's five bucks, everyone wants to trip at the show. It's small, it's easy. It's one of the easiest things to deal with. No one's like—you know, when you sell weed, people look at it and are like, 'This is all right but I've seen better,' and they try to haggle with you. With acid it's a piece of paper. There's no negotiating involved."

I asked him if he worries about undercover cops.

"You walk by someone and you try to get a feel for them as they're walking by and then as they're right next to you, you mumble 'tabs' or 'hits' or 'acid' and you look back and see if they've turned around or not. I don't know, you kind of just have to make a snap decision if they're bastards or if they're cool."

To our left, a group of longhairs works a small grill, cooking four grilled cheeses at a time. One butters the bread, another slaps a slice of cheese on, and another flips the sandwiches, which are coming out lopsided. "What the fuck, it's only a buck!" one of them shouts at people passing by.

Chester's still grooving. Hasn't varied his routine. Mike G, on the other hand, skips around the neighborhood like a cheerleader. He has incredible energy, every limb moving in a different direction, all in sync with the music. Once in a while Mike G ducks into the Blazer to change the disc, and after a few music-less seconds (Chester keeps it going in the lulls—at this point he doesn't need a beat), another gangster rap song cranks over the runway.

Meanwhile, a posse has started to form around Mike G and Chester. The pack of wolves show up. The nose-ringers. The real dregs of this place start flocking here, attracted by the music, which is not Top 40 radio station rap. This is angrier and louder. Mike G starts talking pharmaceuticals to the newcomers.

"It's like we're on Mars," Skins says. He looks stunned. "I feel like we're on another planet where people breathe different air and speak a different language and no one has to follow the normal rules of how you do anything."

For some reason, Chester wanders over this way. His eyes are half-open now. He looks at me and then at Skins. "Mike G that's my boy," he says. "Mike G, he'll hook you up, know what I'm saying? He'll hook you *up*! Each day he wakes up and he's like, 'Hey, Chester, what kind of drugs you wanna do today? What you want Black Beauties? Xanax? blues? reds?' He'll get you spun, Mike G. No matter what, he'll get you spun. He picked me up in Maryland, we went to New York City, you know what I'm talking about? We went to the Renaissance Hotel—*damn*, man! We went to Shea Stadium to see a Yankee game and then out to the strip clubs, and he was dropping *mad* cash. I'm telling you, *mad* cash! We hit Atlantic City—I'm talking about the Taj Mahal. Gambling. Mad cash everywhere!"

I ask Chester what he does.

"I'm a traveler," he says.

About three a.m. Mike G comes over and asks us to watch his stuff—his cooler and all the rest of it, which we can help ourselves to, he says, since we're in the neighborhood. He's going to let the car cool down for a while, take the party on the road and catch us later.

"Tell me your names again, guys," he says, shouldering his boom box. He's flying right now on some terrible cocktail of his own pills, eyes bulging. "I'm terrible with names."

We tell him our names.

"All right. Yeah. I got it. I'm Mike G and that's Chester. But on tour we go by Rock Landers and Chest Rockwell. All right." He turns on his heels, cranks up the music, and with Chester and a growing posse of delinquents heads out into the night.

"What the hell is that?" I say to Skins. "Tour names? Come on. Did you see his eyes?"

"It's from *Boogie Nights,* those names. Two characters from the movie *Boogie Nights.*"

"Oh. Well . . . that's stupid."

We crawl into the tent around four a.m. It's unbearably hot. Even without Mike G in the neighborhood it's loud, like sleeping on a city sidewalk. In the next tent over, a couple is having a vicious fight. The guy mounts a pathetic defense, mumbly and druggy. She's clear as a bell.

"Fuck this!" she yells. "I fucking *hate* it. This is a waste of a fucking month of my summer. I have to go back to school in a fucking *month* and this is not fun at all. Fuck this shit! I'm tired of it. I'm fucking going home tomorrow. I *hate* this tour! This is my last fucking show . . . What?"

"*. . . mumble, mumble . . .*"

"No! Fuck that! I didn't know where you were! You're out doin' Ecstasy all night. I fucking said *don't* do Ecstasy and whadda you do? You fucking do it again the second night in a row! And you're out there selling and you don't fucking care about me! This is *it!* My *last* fucking show!"

In the middle of the fight, Mike G and Chester come back on the scene.

"All right," Mike G says. "Yeah. I'm just going to play a couple of songs." *Ba boom ba boom. . . .*

Chester's voice carries over the music. He's talking to a new girl in the posse, whose name is Butterfly, which Chester can't remember.

"You don't know my name," Butterfly says in a whiny voice.

"Yeah I do."

"What's my name then?"

Silence from Chester.

"If you know it, what *is* it then?"

"What?" Chester says.

"You don't know it. What's my *name?... Chester?*" She sounds like she's probably tugging on his arm to get his attention. ". . . *Chester?*"

I can't take it anymore. I climb out of the tent, at least get some fresh air. A dull white sun is pulling itself up over the runway and a dirty haze hovers over this place and lets no air escape. Steam rises from the earth, probably bubbling beneath the surface. Silhouetted in their tent, the fighting couple is still at it— she's waving her arms wildly and he just sits there like a statue. And over by the dance party, Butterfly really *is* tugging on Chester's arm, and he's still doing that stupid half-dead dance around and around . . . *the bitches, the bitches.* . . . Chester couldn't make it on his own. No way. Without Mike G he'd be in trouble. Totally whacked on who knows what, Mike G jumps around in the morning light, rapping every word to every song that blasts from his Blazer, waking up the neighborhood.

Along the runway, a sewage-pumping truck rumbles by, hissing. It looks like a cement truck. When it stops in front of a row of Porta Potties, two men in jeans and boots jump out. A long plastic tube hangs off the tank and the two men carry it like a giant snake from Porta Potty to Porta Potty, banging open door after door and shoving the snout of the thing down the hole, where it makes a horrible sucking sound. The sewage trucks do most of their work at this time of night, when there aren't lines for every toilet. The men wear yellow rubber gloves, elbow-high. I can't watch them for more than a second.

Drums beat in the distance. The air is sticky and thick and smells of sweat and feces. Mike G's place is hopping.

I crawl back into the tent. This is the low point of the tour. Terrible, terrible, terrible. I can't sleep. I can't use the bathroom—I absolutely refuse to go inside a Porta Potty. I can't even think. I want out of this place. Off this tour. The girl in the next tent over is exactly right: "Fuck this shit."

"This is unbelievable," Skins says, rolled up in a corner of the tent.

I pull out my tape recorder and push the Record button. "Look, if we can't sleep at least maybe we can make some observations. Let's try to get some of this down. Skins, what are your impressions?"

"Um . . . I don't know really . . . it's just . . . I've never seen anything like it."

"Speak up for the recorder."

"I've never seen anything like it . . . it's crazy."

"What else?"

"It's just . . . um . . . insane."

"You're right."

Neither of us can think of anything interesting to note. Usually we point out odd things to each other—you know, "Look over there" or "Check it out." But here, plunked down in the middle of this hellhole, neither of us has anything to say. It's ten times dirtier, nastier, meaner, scarier, than your average Phish show. And who are these teenagers skulking around Mike G's place? I haven't heard one Phish bootleg in the neighborhood, haven't seen one Phish t-shirt, haven't heard any mention of tonight's show or any other show on tour, usually a very hot topic of discussion. I don't think anyone in this nose-ring posse even likes Phish.

By eight o'clock the sun's rays penetrate the tent and we start to roast. I roll off my sweaty sleeping bag and grab my camera. Time to document the carnage. . . . Total wasteland. Half the people didn't even make it inside their tents last night. They lie sprawled on the ground just about everywhere—on the runway, beside a truck's tire, beneath a van, on the hood of a car. It's like at some point last night they ran out of gas and just crumpled wherever they happened to be—facedown on the asphalt. These people are in bad shape: nitrous, Ecstasy, acid coursing through their veins, wearing out as the hours pass, but still holding a nasty grip. One guy lies on his belly beside his guitar, his arms twisted underneath him like a rag doll. He looks dead. Even the fierce sun beating on his pale back won't wake him. An earthquake wouldn't wake him. I lean in close and snap a few pictures.

If a UFO were to land here right now, a hostile UFO looking for new territory, they would return to outer space with a favorable report: *A conquerable people, very aimless and disorganized. They sleep on concrete in the bright sunshine, everywhere, as far as you can see. Recommendation: Attack now.*

It truly does look like a collapsed civilization—trash all around, scruffy people selling their wares and stepping over bodies as they go, a drum beating somewhere in the distance. Some of the older Phishheads are genuinely surprised by this new wave of young kids spinning on all sorts of nasty drugs. You can see it in their eyes as they walk by Mike G's Blazer: What the hell is going on here . . . ?

"A lot of kids are on heavy psychedelic drugs," Johnny Mac said in Burlington. "And enormous cocktails of them. I mean, doing LSD is one thing. Doing Ecstasy is one thing. Doing ketamine, which is this animal tranquilizer, which is a rave drug apparently—I mean, there's some heavy, really fucked-up drugs. Cocaine. And I'm sure there's kids out there on heroin. This is music that people do drugs to. That's the nature of the beast."

The only people awake and moving at this hour are running concessions—the businessmen of the tour. Miles of concessions here, with two main drags converging at one intersection outside the concert venue. One guy in a big straw hat arranges a hundred bongs and pipes on a foldout table. It doesn't look like he's sold very many pieces. Food is the way to go. Even the motley crew frying lopsided grilled cheese last night sold hundreds of sandwiches in a couple of hours. The only shops with business this morning offer breakfast burritos. Burritos of any kind are a hot tour item. With no picnic tables around, you need to be able to walk and eat at the same time, and so most food comes in some kind of a wrap.

I steer clear of the breakfast burritos. I'm trying to eat as little as possible at Oswego in a serious effort to avoid Porta Potties, which are indescribably awful even with the tanker guys working around the clock. A friend of mine had a terrible experience in one. He ate some mushrooms and then a little while later he stepped into a Porta Potty. It was overflowing, he said, but he had already started, you know, too hard to stop. So he said to himself, Stay calm, a few more seconds. . . . He walked out, took a deep breath, and projectile-vomited in the direction of a garbage can.

I'm feeling a bit light-headed with no food in my stomach, but it's worth it. Best to stay on the move. Along the runway I meet another guy snapping pictures, except he has a big lens and doesn't have to sneak up on passed-out people. He seems a bit shell-shocked by the scene. "It's a different crowd than the Dead crowd," he says. "The other day we woke up to gangster rap and this teenager was like, 'Let's go sell some coke.'" His name is Douglass and he's here to shoot the event for a stock photography house in New York City. Hardly anyone's covering it in the press, he says, and so he thinks he can make some money with these pictures, selling here and there to magazines calling up for artwork. He's an old Deadhead, even though he's just twenty-five, which probably means he started seeing Dead shows maybe ten years ago, which is a long time in rock and roll.

I ask him why he comes to Phish shows.

"It's a stress reliever. Everybody here wants to be a clown. You can't do this in normal life. You can't walk around New York City or whatever with bells on your head—at least you can't if you

want to get a loan and have a house and all that. But here you can do it. You can be a clown."

I head down the runway to "Camp Oswego"—a grassy field with giant marshmallow objects waving in the air. The marshmallows are made of cloth, as big as a beanbag chair, stuck on top of birch saplings scattered around the field. The theme to this year's artwork is "Camp"—giant paper lanterns lighting the way, logs for benches, huts made of sticks. A sinister theme, camp, since the absolute last thing in the world happening here is a Boy Scout roasting of marshmallows over an open fire.

Each year, for the last few summers, there has been an artistic theme to the big weekend party. Artists and sculptors, hired by the band, work on large projects right beside the venue. Last year in Maine, at Lemonwheel, they created a Japanese Garden with pagodas and huts and waterfalls. A team of landscapers with bulldozers worked for weeks, transforming acres of the flat landscape into a hilly terrain of streams and ponds. In the middle of the garden stood a six-story pagoda, which from a distance looked, well, Japanese, until you got up close and realized the structure

was made of blue Porta Potties stacked on top of one another—
the Porta Potty Pagoda. The first-level door had to be locked
because some fans had thought it was just like any other Porta
Potty. The artist behind it all, Lars-Erik Fisk, has a pretty good
deal. For the past few years, he's been the art director for the big
summer shows. The band throws loads of money his way, hires
landscapers, carpenters, whatever Lars-Erik needs, and basically
says, "Okay, go for it, do whatever you want." Lars-Erik is in his
late twenties and part of the Burlington art scene—lives in a first-
floor apartment in town, hangs around artists, wears t-shirts that
are too small. His studio is in an old warehouse down by the lake,
near the office of Phish's management, Dionysian Productions.

"In my art I like the awesome reality of a thing, its sheer size,"
Lars-Erik told me. "But at the same time it's an absolutely absurd
subject. In these shows I'm able to push this notion of the absurd,
almost preposterously wrong. Rather than just appropriate the
design of a Japanese garden, I wanted to push it into something
else. I don't like to say this, but I like to pervert things. I'm taking
elements of ancient tradition and making them Americanized."

Camp Oswego isn't quite as elaborate as last year's Japanese
garden. Not as much money or time invested, apparently because
the band is saving up for some spectacular New Year's Eve set.
The huts seem to be quite popular at Camp Oswego, with a few
Phishheads hiding inside, peering out through the little holes,
maybe having a bad trip.

Back in the neighborhood, Mike G and Chester have finally
reached the end of the line. They sleep, open-mouthed, in the
back of the Blazer with the hatch flipped up. Skins and I crack
open some beer and take our post on the Jimmy. At high noon
the drug selling is completely out of hand—dealers holding up
their drugs in broad daylight, weaving through the crowds. I've
never seen this at a show before, never so out in the open.

"It's like Sodom and Gomorrah," Skins says. "Fire and brimstone is going to rain down on this place."

"Yeah. That's probably true."

(I didn't know what he meant, but I didn't want to admit it, him being my younger brother. So I looked it up in the encyclopedia later, which said that Sodom and Gomorrah were "notoriously sinful cities in the Old Testament Book of Genesis." Near Israel, except supposedly they are buried underwater because of an earthquake in the Dead Sea—God's retribution, his fire and brimstone, for the cities' wickedness. Sexual acts of a certain nature were also rampant throughout Sodom. . . .)

We end up chatting with a high-school student named Lisa from Plattsburg, New York. Her tent is next to ours. She's been on tour for a while and can't quite believe this scene.

"I used to like going to Phish shows," she says. "But now I don't know. The music's great, but I don't know. . . . You have to be on your toes now."

"What did you think of the rap party last night?" I say.

She rolls her eyes. "I actually slept through most of it, I think."

"And how about that fight? Did you hear that couple last night?"

"I don't think so."

"How could you not? 'Fuck *this*, I'm going home, what the fuck—' "

"Oh yeah. I heard that." She looks over her shoulder. "Those are the people I'm doing the tour with. They do that all the time. Practically every night. And then everything's normal again in the morning."

At two p.m. Chester stirs in the back of the Blazer. I've been keeping one eye on them all afternoon, because what else is there to do? He stumbles off to the bathroom. While he's gone, a scuzzy-looking dude with a cut-up face and a bruised lip climbs in the back of the Blazer and curls up next to Mike G. A minute later Chester comes back, sees that his spot has been taken, and doesn't know what to do. He stands there for a second, swaying. He's confused. *Was Bruised Lip there the whole time? Did we all sleep together back there?* Chester sits down on the cooler and looks around the neighborhood, bewildered. It's like he's never seen the place before. *Where are we? What the hell is going on?* He folds his arms on the back of the Blazer and lays his head down beside Mike G's sneakers.

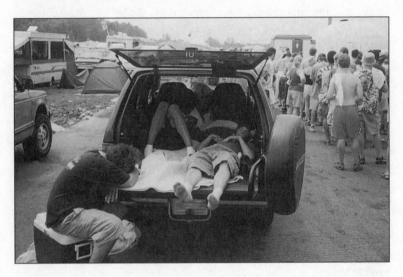

Bruised Lip is the first one to move. He sits straight up. Like Chester, he has no idea what's happening, where he is, etc. This guy looks terrible. Beat up and swollen. He stares at Mike G's long, stretched-out legs. He stares at Chester on the cooler. He takes his hat off, rubs his blood-crusted face with both hands, and puts his hat back on. He stands, takes a few unsure steps towards us, red-eyed, and says, "Nuggets." He staggers down the runway. "Nuggets . . . Nuggets . . ."

The brazenness of the drug selling is extremely surprising. Plenty of people have been arrested on this tour already. I've seen Phishheads asking for donations to help get a buddy out of jail. I saw one woman crying after a show, begging people for money. Most Phishheads know about mandatory minimum laws. They know that people get busted. They know that if you're busted with LSD on a sugar cube you're screwed, because sugar weighs more than paper, and jail time hinges on weight. Some of them,

I'm sure, have heard of the book *Shattered Lives*, which tells the story of Deadheads behind bars serving mandatory minimums, which in some states are brutal even for first-time offenders. But no one here gives a shit about that. It's another planet, Skins is right. Another planet where tomorrow is light years away. Planet Oswego that has been handed over to Phishheads for the weekend and everyone else has taken the fuck off.

Security at these big events is a joke—a t-shirt crew of teenagers and buzz-cut college football players whose instructions seem to be "Take it easy." Last summer at Lemonwheel I ran into one guy I know working security, and when he spotted my backstage pass he said, "Yo, dude, you got an extra one of those?"

I'm not sure what the deal is exactly with security. At these big events I think Phish says to the airport people, Okay, clear out, give us this place and we'll bring in our own security team—don't worry about a thing. There's one dude who I've seen around these shows over the years working security. Usually in a blue EVENT STAFF or SECURITY t-shirt and a pair of jeans, he stands around taking in the scene, chatting with whoever comes across his path. He's a little guy with a big mustache, about forty, and he once introduced himself to me as "Highway." He's pretty serious about his job, though I've never actually seen him in action—i.e., stopping anyone from doing anything.

"I tell people who haven't worked this type of thing before, 'Watch out when the people come,'" Highway said, arms folded across his chest. "When you see so many people coming, you don't know what to do." He looked across the venue and nodded his head. "I remember my first concert, man. Peter Frampton, Madison Square Garden. Sold out. With my mom."

Mike G wakes up late in the afternoon. He strolls around the neighborhood.

"You had some company back there," I say.

"Who?"

"Some guy, real beat up, slept next to you for a while."

"Oh no!" Mike G says. "That fucker. He's nasty, all cut up? I hope he wasn't bleeding on my pillow. Was he bleeding?"

"He, ah, looked pretty bad."

"Shit! That guy is nasty. Yeah, he got beat up last night. These dudes kicked the shit out of him. He owed them money and he was trying to avoid them, but they found him last night. Damn! He was sleeping with me?"

"Curled right up."

"Guy's nasty!"

Bruised Lip has left a cardboard box behind, tucked under the Blazer. It's full of puppies—tiny suckers crawling all over each other. No one around Mike G's place knows where Bruised Lip is right now or what he plans to do with the puppies or why the hell he has them. My theory is that when he runs through his nugget sales he's going to hock the puppies on tour in order to pay back whoever kicked his butt.

We head to the show about six p.m. No seats here, just a big field, and a lot of people have arrived before us. Phish is four dots on stage. You have to be committed to get up close. The first-rowers have to run for it when the gate opens. It's a scary sight—a barefoot hungover mob running across an empty field, grim-faced and determined to get there, no matter the cramp knifing their ribs. It's by far the most exercise anyone gets on tour. When they reach the stage they drop to the ground, gasping for air. Then, a minute later, as they realize how close they made it to the stage, they stand up and raise their hands in victory, hours before the show starts.

Back here there's plenty of room. A few people are getting a little out of hand with the dancing, twirling blindly in a trance, bumping into one another. I pick a spot next to a pretty mellow group smoking pot. They pass around a pipe and hug each other. I stretch out in a patch of grass beside them and fall asleep soundly.

Bit o' France

July 19, Niagara Falls, New York

I dropped my brother off at the Syracuse airport at eight a.m. He was glad as hell to get off the tour. For the past couple of days he's been worried that he would miss his Monday morning flight because we didn't have an alarm clock. "I don't know how we're going to make it," he kept saying.

"I think Mike G and Chester will keep us up," I said. "You'll make it."

And he did. He slung his bag over his shoulder, gave me a final wave, and walked very quickly through the doors of the Delta terminal.

I drove into downtown Syracuse to meet my Vermont friend Dan, who's coming along for the next leg of the tour. I saw Dan briefly yesterday at Oswego. He was flying on mushrooms. Big smile, sunburned face, drinking gin from a plastic coffee mug, laughing about this and that. He was about as happy as a person could be, and he wore this blue Hawaiian shirt with white ferns. "I love Oswego!" he said. "I love Oswego!" He took me to his camping spot, which he was very proud of, right beside the sinister "Camp Oswego" entrance. I asked him how he landed there and he said, "A friend of mine knows this guy. . . ." About half of Dan's sentences start with "A friend of mine knows this guy. . . ." Vermont is a small state, and if you've lived there for a while your friends know just about every guy around.

Dan is a big Phish fan. He's been on tour before, even hitch-hiked through snowstorms to catch the holiday shows when he was in high school. He sold grilled cheese on tour for extra cash. He's definitely the biggest Phish fan that I know personally. Recently, his house was robbed and the burglar took all his Phish bootlegs. "Some of those tapes are irreplaceable," he said. "I could literally kill that guy." I'm not going to mention what Dan does for work, or his last name, because, well, he doesn't want me to. He says he'd rather keep the whole thing with the book low pro- file, since you don't know who's going to read it. He parties like a rock star and consumes quantities of liquor and drugs that would instantly put me back in the hospital. Never gets a hangover, either. One of these guys who can party until dawn, crash for a few hours, and have a drink in his hand again by noon. He trav- els to Phish shows in crowded Subarus with people named Ram- sey and Cosmo and Grey (hippie Vermont parents) who eat organically grown carrots and broccoli in the back of the car while Dan looks hopefully out the window at the passing Burger King. Nothing makes him happier than going to Phish shows. He runs into all sorts of people there—some he's psyched to see, and some he'll spot and say, "That bastard's here . . . I hate that guy. Drove to the Philly shows with him year before last." He doesn't always remember what happens at shows. He never remembers set lists. The next day if you remind him of something that hap- pened the night before, he'll say, "Wait . . . when was that?" Which is strange because he has a near-photographic memory otherwise. As a young kid, Dan was enrolled in some kind of advance study program for gifted children where you go off to college in the summer to study calculus with other little boy and girl geniuses. In the seventh grade he was scoring higher on tests than most high school seniors.

Dan lives in Burlington in a small apartment with a guy named Marty who owns a Chihuahua. The Chihuahua is out of control, craps all over the place, yaps every morning. Dan hates it. Nearly every weekend they throw a rager which goes until dawn. People Dan has never seen before show up, and often the party lasts two days. Actually, they can even last three days, depending on beer supply, with naps here and there. On those weekends, Dan barely steps outside. Just the thought of his weekend party, on a Wednesday or a Thursday, makes him smile and reach into his shirt pocket for a Marlboro. By the time the party is in full swing on Friday night, he's laughing and shouting and drinking. If someone turns on the television it makes him mad. He hates TV (except for *The Simpsons*) and thinks it ruins parties. "It's terrible," he says. "Everyone sits down and stares at it." So he turns off the TV and cranks up the stereo and tries to keep Marty off the music selection, since Marty's taste runs toward Top 40, which Dan simply cannot tolerate. It makes him shiver with anger. Dan will throw on Stevie Wonder or Al Green, nod his head, and walk back towards the crowd. "Stevie's the man," he says.

On Monday morning he climbs back into his old Volvo, lights a cigarette, and heads to work. He looks pretty grim on Monday morning. Almost angry. The weekend's over, the place is a mess, and he's low on smokes since people were bumming one after the other all weekend long. And he needs gas. He puts on a Phish bootleg and zones out for a while, wondering if Marty's going to write down his phone messages for once or if the Chihuahua will somehow get into his bedroom despite the padlock.

When I asked Dan to come on tour with me this summer, he said, "Yeah, I'll go. It'll be my paid vacation."

I asked him why he likes going to shows so much.

"When you're at a Phish show you're just totally lost, dancing as hard as you can," he said. "You're not thinking about anything else. My mind pretty much goes blank. It's nice to give your brain a rest. Sometimes I'll get distracted and think about things, but when I'm really having a great, great time it feels like the music is flowing right through my head. I think that's one of the reasons I don't remember a lot of the songs after the show. Like I can tell if I haven't had a really good time if I can remember all the songs. Drugs could have something to do with it from time to time. But I've done it sober. All you're doing is looking at the

lights and them playing and dancing uncontrollably, just like
jumping up and down and spinning around and flailing your
arms and totally not self-conscious about anything, because the
guy next to you is so much crazier than you are and they just
don't care. You're looking up there, looking up at the sky or spinning around looking at the lights bouncing off the walls. Like in a
club sometimes you can get self-conscious or whatever because
there's girls there, or that guy's a better dancer, but at a Phish
show there's not a mandated dance. You can get crazy."

We have a day off today, thank God. No show tonight. After
Oswego everyone needs a break. So we're headed to Niagara Falls, a three-hour drive.

"I haven't been there since I was a kid," Dan says.

"Yeah, this is a good plan," I say. "We'll find a motel close by,
maybe catch a movie. I'd like to do something normal, you know.
Something that has nothing to do with Phish."

"Fine with me. A movie sounds good."

Along the highway, we pass a lot of Phishheads going in the
same direction.

"I bet a bunch of fans are headed to Niagara," I say. "It's sort of
on the way."

"It would be a good place to go if you wanted to finish up your
drugs before the border crossing," Dan says.

"Yeah. You could look at the crashing water all day."

Tomorrow night's show is in Toronto. There's been a lot of talk
on tour about the border crossing—stories of vans raided and
stripped in years past, massive fines and arrests. I've heard that
some fans are skipping Toronto altogether.

We pull into a rest stop and talk with a guy doing the tour by
himself. He's repacking his car.

"Hey, what do you know about the border crossing?" he
asks me.

"Not much, really. I've heard some things. Dan, what do you
know about the border?"

"Basically, they can search your whole car without reason, strip it down, and leave it by the side of the road."

"No shit?" the guy says. "I'm thinking about going to Buffalo and leaving my stash in a locker and then picking it up when I come back."

"Yeah?" Dan says.

"Probably smart," I say.

As we merge back on the highway, I all of a sudden wonder if Dan has brought any drugs along for the border crossing. I have a vision of the Jimmy torn apart while some red-jacketed Canadian in a felt hat reads us the riot act, with the U.S. marshals on the way.

"So, ah, Dan . . . you got anything stashed away for the crossing?"

"You mean drugs?"

"Yeah. Drugs. You know, rolled up in the sleeping bag?"

"No. I got rid of it all at Oswego."

"Good man."

"I don't want any hassle at the border," Dan says. "This guy I know got in trouble once."

"What happened?"

"He had some pot on him, not that much. Fined two hundred bucks. It was a big pain in the ass. So I don't want any hassle at the border. I brought a collared shirt just for the occasion."

"Perfect. I'll wear my glasses. They'll wave us right on through."

"Yeah, they will."

Niagara, the town, is an ugly place. Gas station after gas station, motels everywhere, souvenir shops with neon arrows: STOP HERE! OFFICIAL NIAGARA FALLS GIFT SHOP. Everything looks rundown. The rain doesn't help. I pull into a motel with an empty parking lot—the Bit o' France. The sign says, ONE ROOM $29.99.

"Good. We'll save some money tonight."

"I don't know about this place," Dan says.

"It'll be fine. How bad could it be?"

All the rooms face the parking lot and only one room is taken. The door is open and two Phishheads peer out at us. Both are shirtless and scraggly—classic Shaggy characters. They seem to be a bit spooked. One of them sticks his head out for a second, spots us, then ducks back in. The light is off in their room and they watch us from the darkness, standing beside the bed. I doubt they will make it to the waterfall.

No Best Western, this place. No VW Jettas in the parking lot plastered with Phish stickers. In the motel lobby, a short Indian man with a turban hands me the room key. "Six," he says. "Over there." He points to the room next door to the Phish dudes.

As we unpack, they close the door halfway and watch us through the window. They don't even seem to be talking to one another. The television isn't on. No sound comes from their room.

"This place is nasty," Dan says.

I pull down the bed covers to inspect the sheets. Stained and hairy.

"This isn't going to work out," I say to the turbaned man back in the lobby. "The room isn't clean."

"Oh no, sir. What is problem?"

"The sheets are dirty."

"Impossible. What room number? Was cleaned already today, just now."

"Well, it's dirty and I want my money back."

"No-money-back policy, sir. See this here—I can't do that." He pulls out the rules and slides them across the counter.

A worn-out, weary-looking guy with dead eyes comes out of the backroom carrying a towel. The turbaned man turns to him. "I thought number six *clean* you said!"

"It is," the towel guy mumbles. "I just cleaned six."

"I am *very* embarrassed," he says, turning back to me. "I am very embarrassed."

The towel guy notices me standing there for the first time. He's confused.

"Listen," I say, "just give me my money back and we'll forget—"

"I can't do that! Come, sir, follow me. I can't give money back,
sir. What room are you? I give you new room. Follow me. Very
clean. Come with me. Please understand, sir. Come with me."

He fumbles with a large set of keys as we walk across the parking lot in the gray drizzle. He walks quickly and glances over his
shoulder at me, very anxious. The two silent Phishheads peer out
the window, retreating into the darkness as we approach.

The second room smells a little better.

"You see?" the man says. "*Very* nice!"

I go to the bed and pull down the covers. Stains on the sheet.
And a few curly hairs.

"No," I say. "Look at this."

He looks at the sheet and then at me. "I don't see nothing, sir."

"Well, what is *that*?" I point at the mess. He won't look down
at the bed again. "I want my money back."

He points a bony finger at me.

"You, sir, are very picky! *Very picky*! Only a five-star hotel for
you! Nothing pleases you!"

"I don't like stains on my sheets."

"GO, THEN! To a five-star hotel! Nothing else satisfies you!
Very bad customer!"

"Yeah, that's what I plan to do. Find a five-star hotel with clean
sheets." But at this point he's out the door, marching back to the
lobby, waving his hands above his head and yelling in another
language.

Across the counter, he pushes my cash at me, cursing as I leave,
the towel guy still standing there bewildered. The sounds of a
very odd porno movie drift into the lobby from the backroom.

Pulling out of the parking lot, I notice one of the Phishheads,
half-hidden behind the curtain, watching us drive away.

A mile down the road we spot the Best Western. Perfect. So
what if it's twice as much money. Clean sheets, nicely wrapped

bars of soap, fluffy towels. In the lobby I see a couple of well-groomed fans. Yes, sir.

I explain to the desk clerk that we came from the Bit 'o France down the road.

He recently fired a cleaning woman who used to work the small-motel circuit around here, he tells me. "She wouldn't change the sheets. She said they didn't do it at her old place. So we fired her."

"Good."

"Here's the key. Second floor, top of the stairs."

My favorite moment of life on the road: clicking the hotel door open, seeing two beds perfectly made up, and flopping down on top of the covers. I smell the air freshener, hear the hum of the AC, stretch my arms and legs as far as they go. Okay, here we are, I think. Then I go check out the bathroom. See how many towels we have, pick up the mini shampoo bottles, tear the paper wrap off the toilet and jump-shot it into the empty garbage can. Then I investigate the TV channel selection. Almost all the chain motels have HBO. It's pretty standard. They might only have five or six other channels, but everyone has HBO. If they didn't have HBO, I'd probably call up and complain. Once in a while, we'll watch the news for a minute or two. I'm totally disconnected from the rest for the world and have no idea what's going on. Newspapers, forget it. Occasionally, I'll pick up *USA Today*, glance at the top stories, and flip to the Hollywood Report. All the other newspapers on the road are local, with the front-page headline from the state fair—world news doesn't penetrate into the belly of America. There's really no need for world news on tour. People talk about last night's show, the best route to the next venue, and what they think Phish will open up with tonight.

"I like this place," Dan says, propping up the pillows on his bed. With the remote, he clicks on Jerry Springer.

I turn on my laptop and take some notes before we hit Niagara Falls. It's hard writing with Springer in the background. Hard to resist watching. Lacey the hooker, whose real name is Kim, is having it out with her mom and daughter, who both want her to quit prostituting, pronto, and get a regular job. Lacey doesn't want to quit, what with all the cash she makes and the flexible lifestyle. With one hand on his forehead and the other white-knuckled around the mike, Jerry keeps saying to Lacey, "I can't *believe* this. This is *crazy*. Don't you *love* your daughter?"

We make it to the falls at seven p.m. Phishheads crawling all over the place. Tons of Japanese tourists mixed in too, video cameras perched on their shoulders recording the Phishheads along with the waterfall. What must these Japanese think? *Who are these wild creatures? Do they live near the waterfall?* There are some Hardcores here, not just the preppies in baseball caps. Barefoot dudes with dreadlocks down to their waist sit on the benches and stare out over the edge. Maybe Dan was right. Maybe this is the place to come to gobble up the last of your stash before the border crossing.

It's always strange seeing Phishheads away from the Phish scene. I should be used to it by now, since every time we have a night off we run into whole packs of them wherever we go. But

outside the context of Phish, you realize how incredibly weird
these people look and how alien they must appear to the rest of
the society. What do people think when they see a gang of dirty
ragged young people with matted hair and no shoes walking
about, or driving down the highway, or swarming Niagara Falls?
Most people stop and stare, then move on. Phishheads know that
people have this reaction. They know they are an odd bunch. But
that's okay. More than okay, in fact. That's part of it—living on
the fringe, in search of something different.

The crashing water makes a pretty good roar. It kicks up a
misty cloud that floats downriver. Below the waterfall, the river
is bright green, almost Caribbean, with long streaks of white
foam. Way down below us, sightseeing boats motor along
towards the waterfall and they nose right up to the edge of the
destruction zone. The waterfall itself isn't that impressive. I had
expected something much higher. It's wide all right, but that's
not exciting, the width of the thing. Our lookout spot isn't even
that close to the actual falls. I expected to sidle right up next to
the wall of water, maybe see someone go over in a barrel. It's
hard to believe this was once the big honeymoon spot. It's not
particularly romantic. Nothing private about this place. The tumbling water gets old after a few minutes, and then what else is
there to do for the rest of the honeymoon?

The Sloth

July 20, Toronto, Canada

Approaching the border in the Jimmy. For the first time of the trip, in five MPH traffic, Dan buckles up. With the seatbelt strapped smartly across his chest and his collared shirt buttoned to the neck, Dan looks . . . presentable. Even his furry goatee is smoothed out. The backseat of the Jimmy is neat and ordered, the camping gear tucked away, all empty bottles chucked at the last rest stop.

With the checkpoint station a few feet away, Dan seems a bit nervous.

"I just want it to be hassle free," he says. He looks over at a car beside us, waiting in line. It's a blue Volvo full of Phishheads sitting up straight, trying their best to look upstanding, a difficult task with dreadlocks and tangled necklaces and the smell of patchouli wafting out the windows.

"If they have a choice between us and them, we're safe," Dan says. He thinks about that for a second and nods to himself.

We roll up to the gate.

"Do you have any weapons, guns, or firearms?" a sharp-featured customs woman says. She sounds annoyed.

"No."

"Mace or pepper spray?"

"No."

"Anything other than personal clothing?"

"No."

"Where were you born?"

A few more questions and we're through.

"No problem," Dan says, unbuttoning his top two buttons. He turns up the radio. "*Noooo* problem."

We stop for lunch at Subway. A few Canadian-style fast-food joints right next door, but why take a chance? On line we meet Mike and Aaron, two Canadian factory workers also getting foot-long subs for the ride to the show tonight. They ask us about the summer tour's highlights and seem quite impressed that I'm doing the whole tour.

"Yup," I say. "Started in Kansas a few weeks back."

"I'd like to see more shows," Mike says, "but, you know, the money." Mike is tall and freckled, with long red hair and friendly eyes. "I saw my first show at the Niagara Falls Expo Center a few years ago," he says. "Through word of mouth, you know. I saw it and I was just . . . wow! I've seen about a dozen shows since then. I'm excited for tonight. Toronto should be good."

I ask him if Phish is big in Toronto, and he says yeah, pretty big.

From the front of the line, Aaron looks back at us. He's been watching the woman behind the counter make his sandwich. "Did you hear what happened at the border last night?" he asks us, glancing down at his Subway club piled with lettuce and tomatoes.

"No."

"The band," he says. "They were held up at the border."

"No shit."

"Un-uh. No shit. They stopped the bus. My sister, she works for customs, yeah? They detained the bus at customs for hours."

"What did they find?" I say.

"She wasn't sure exactly, but something. They were all just walking around, the band, outside the bus, my sister said. And I said, 'Shit, you should have called me! I would've come down to say hey, you know.'"

"But they made it through?" Dan says.

"Oh, yeah. They let them through, but after a long search."

On the way out, Mike and Aaron say they'll look for us tonight in Toronto and they hope we have a great time. They give us a big wave. It's a stereotype, I know, but Canadians are so . . . something. Earnest? Sincere? A bit naive maybe? These guys are by far the nicest, most unguarded fans I've met on tour so far.

Driving into downtown Toronto, I get the feeling I have whenever I'm out of the United States. Uncomfortable. Nervous. I don't like traveling in other countries. It's hard to understand signs, people, menus, everything. It's all unfamiliar, and it makes me miss the U.S.A. And I've only been gone a few hours. Toronto is a nice city—tall buildings of blue glass, not much traffic, public parks scattered all over the place with men in ties and women in skirts eating lunch, chatting, faces pointed towards the sun. Not a bad scene, really. Just not home.

"Which way should I go?"

"It doesn't matter," Dan says. "Just park and we'll walk around. I saw a bar with a second-story terrace I'd like to check out." Dan's getting thirsty.

Phishheads everywhere you look, mingling with the businessmen. Not a particularly crowded city, so a few thousand Phishheads roaming the streets at three p.m. on a sunny afternoon make a visible impact. One bar, right in the heart of downtown, with a streetside patio, is full of fans crowded around small tables drinking beer. This is a great feeling, maybe one of the best in the world—sitting on a bar patio, sun in the sky, pint in hand, Phish tickets tucked safely inside your wallet.

In the parking lot before the show a Canadian named Shane offers up margaritas. He has a working bar in his trunk.

"I'll take one," Dan says.

Not long after, Dan stands there gabbing away, one set of fingers gripping Shane's bottle of Cuervo, the other wrapped around Shane's bottle of tequila mix. He's pouring his third or fourth extremely stiff drink when he drains the last of Shane's mix.

"Shane, ah, I'm really sorry," Dan says, mortified. "But I, ah, just finished the mix bottle. I didn't know . . . I'm just—"

"I've got another," Shane says, pulling a green bottle from the trunk.

Dan and Shane are fast buddies, talking about this and that. At one point a pretty girl in a long dress, skipping, asks Dan if he has an extra beer. He sure does, he says, and hands over a bottle. No one in this margarita crowd can find a bottle opener, so Dan pries it open with his teeth, which wins a big hug from the pretty girl, except that at the moment she lifts her tan arms to throw them around his neck, at that very moment, Dan—and everyone else sipping margaritas—notices the thick tufts of hair in the pits, extremely dark. He flinches for a second, in the embrace, and keeps a bit of distance by arching his back.

Inside the show, Dan spends most of the first set on the move. He comes back from each trip with a draft Molson in a large paper cup, nodding his head as he walks quickly down the aisle. On one of his trips, he misses one of his favorite tunes: "Sloth."

They call me the Sloth . . . the song begins. The Sloth is an evil character in the land of Gamehendge, a make-believe land that exists in Phish songs. Knights, rebels, spies, wizards, hangmen, inhabit Gamehendge—along with evil Wilson, King of Lizards, who plagues the journey of Colonel Forbin in his search for the Helping Friendly Book. One day, while shaving, bored with his life on earth, Colonel Forbin walks through a door into Gamehendge and the adventure begins. The Gamehendge songs form the core of early Phish tunes from the mid-1980s, and the diehard fans are always waiting for *that* night—there's only been two or three so far, the last in 1994—the night where the band plays the whole Gamehendge saga.

Gamehendge was Trey's senior thesis at Goddard College in Vermont. In the mid-eighties Trey and Fishman transferred from UVM to join Page at Goddard, a progressive college south of Burlington with a couple hundred students, many of whom are writers, artists, musicians. The actor William H. Macy and the writer David Mamet are Goddard grads—their senior theses tucked away in the library in the same section with other well-

known alumni. But according to the librarian, the Phish theses
are by far the most asked for—fans make the trip, particularly in
the spring. You're not allowed to check them out, but you can
can sit and read them at the table. "One guy even had his mom
take a picture of him while he was holding the thesis," the librarian said.

Ellen Codling, director of admissions at Goddard, said that
Phish has brought some students to the school. "It comes up
sometimes in interviews," Codling said. "We always ask, 'Where
did you hear about the college?' Sometimes they say Phish. It's
not a huge magnet, but it's a factor. I wouldn't want to say that
it's bringing them in faster than we can handle."

Dan has partied at Goddard. Last time, things were looking
pretty good with a certain coed, something about a moonlit walk
and a patch of grass, and then everything going horribly wrong
because he lost his wallet and then his keys and had to retrace his
steps around the campus, including his steps out to the nice patch
of grass by the edge of the woods. He's always losing things. At
Phish shows he loses his shoes—it's a constant problem. So it's
no surprise he ran into trouble in the dark, woodsy Goddard College campus.

"Pretty good parties there," Dan said. "But small. Security
only works during the day. RAs don't live in the dorms—I don't
even think they live on campus. My friend was telling me one
time he was sitting around and these two kids from Montpelier
were there who don't go to Goddard and they were smoking a
bowl in the common room and the RA walked in with an
announcement or something and the Montpelier kid passed the
RA the bowl and he was like, 'Nah. I'm all set.' He let him keep
smoking while he made the announcement."

I can't believe I missed 'Sloth,'" Dan says, walking back to his
seat, Molson spilling over the brim. Later in the set, Phish covers Led Zeppelin's "Misty Mountain Hop." They've never played
this before, perhaps further evidence of border trouble last night:

Just then a policeman stepped up to me asked us said,
Please hey would we care to all get in line. . . .

After the show, things are pretty quiet in the parking lot. This
is one of the few venues on the summer tour that wasn't sold out.
Even so, there are traffic jams and thousands of people roaming
around, a few fireworks here and there. But it's not bursting at
the seams like usual. I've started to take it for granted—one sold-
out show after the next, one crazy scene after the next, thousands
and thousands of people *without* tickets, wandering around
before showtime, hoping to get in, searching for a ticket. But you
know, this is not normal. This is not standard in rock and roll.
Phish is one in a million. This scene is one in a million.

I asked Sam Ankerson, the Strangefolk guy, to explain Phish's
success. I asked him what was the smartest thing they did from a
business standpoint.

"I don't know," he said. "They've always seemed to have a
very good understanding of themselves and of their direction.
You can tell in the music it's obvious that they're confident. They
did something that when you first heard it was totally off the
wall, and now to the surprise of all of us everyone's into it. Trey
wrote this Gamehendge thing in college. The concept has been
there from the beginning, and it's been handled so well—it's
never been watered down in any way, never been compromised
in any way. They've never caved in to any kind of commercial
pressure to make a more accessible radio song. They've always
insisted on doing it their way and have done a very good job of it.
Also from their business standpoint, they've hired great people.
And not too many of them. The Grateful Dead got into trouble—
they hired all their friends and wound up having this enormous
overhead of people they just had to support. From what I've
heard, people work to death over there [at Phish headquarters in
Burlington]. People have more work than they can do. So I don't
know about the single best business move. Just confidence in
everything. Knowing when to take those steps into bigger arenas,

knowing that people are going to come and knowing the music is going to back it up and knowing they're going to blow away everyone in the place. Once, I think it was in '93, the Dead were doing ten nights or whatever at the Boston Garden and Phish set up a three-night stand in Worcester or someplace like that. And everyone was like, 'What the fuck are you doing?' And they were like, 'Whatever. We don't care.' And they fucking sold out their shows."

"Do you still go to shows?" I said.

"I don't really go to Phish shows anymore. When I was going to a lot of Phish shows it was because I thought they were fucking awesome. I was blown away by the fact that they never fucked up, I had never heard songs like this before, and I was craving the peak. But now I'm essentially, at least compared to everyone I hang out with, I'm sober. And I also stopped seeing Phish very abruptly. It was New Year's '94. It was the lyrics again. I was just like, 'I can't do this anymore, this is fucking stupid.' Honestly, that's what I thought to myself. And I didn't go back."

Bars close early in Toronto. The whole city shuts down, turns off the lights, and there's really nobody around, which pisses Dan off because at this point he's ready to get things started. We end up at a place called the Pita Put, a small deli with a young guy, maybe twenty-two, making pitas. None of the Pita Put's customers at two a.m. have heard of Phish. They think I'm kidding around, four or five hiply-dressed Canadians with black shoes and Levi's, probably just coming out of the clubs. They think I'm joking about following this band Phish all over the place.

"They were at the Molson Amphitheatre tonight, just down the road," I say. "Didn't you see the millions of weirdos walking around today in the city?"

Ha ha ha . . . there weren't any weirdos walking around Toronto today, they say, stepping up to order their pitas.

At the front of the line, Dan is getting in trouble. He leans on the counter, his pita on a paper plate, demanding French fries.

"Fries are on the way," the pita maker says with a grin. "Just another minute or two." He winks at the Canadians. There is no fryer on the premises, which Dan doesn't believe, even though I've told him this over and over.

"Yeah there *is*," he says. "The guy says the fries are coming. I'm telling you there's fries. . . . Hey, how are those fries coming?"

"Right along," the pita maker says. I don't know how this got started. It's like the dark side of the Mr. Nice Guy Canadian routine, an unclever sarcasm that only works on brain-clouded drunks. What the pita maker doesn't get is that Dan doesn't think it's funny, and that he's consumed, at this point, enormous quantities of Shane's tequila and maybe eight or nine beers and that he is completely determined to get fries, thinks he already paid for them. "The guy said fries are included in the price," Dan tells me, watching the pita maker carefully.

I step outside and eat my pita. Through the glass, I see Dan jabbering on and on, the pita maker occasionally looking up with a smirk. I can't hear anything with the door closed, but it's clear things are heating up when the Doc Martened club-hopping Canadians at the counter glance at one another, frowning. The pita maker is starting to look a bit pale . . . *What kind of strange American have I got on my hands?* . . . Dan isn't exactly big, but he's got some girth, and you get the feeling that he could do a lot of damage in a very short amount of time, and that he would go down hard.

I walk back in and tug Dan out by the arm, who at this point is yelling for fries and glaring at the pita maker, who smiles nervously and keeps saying—because now he's in too deep and can't back down in his own deli—"Coming right up! One order of fries!"

I've got a firm grip on Dan and we head down the street.

"Look, we've got to find a hotel," I say. "Forget about that guy."

We head towards the Holiday Inn, one of the fanciest hotels in downtown Toronto, much more impressive than the U.S. Holiday Inns. This one is a tall white building as big as a city block with some nice penthouses on the top floors. No rooms anywhere else in the city. This is it, the last chance for a bed. (Earlier, we stepped into another fancy hotel with checkered marble floors and mirrors everywhere and Egyptian statues and a glossy lobby through which a greasy Phishhead drifted whispering, "Mushrooms.")

Dan looks up at the Holiday Inn. "*This* is the place to stay. That's what I'm *talking* about."

"I bet the band stays here," I say.

"Yeah, I could see that. Definitely. I'll go check it out."

"Here," I say, handing him my tape recorder. "Take this. Push the Record button when you get inside."

He comes back a few minutes later waving the *Globe and Mail* newspaper, shouting the headline RAZOR RUDDOCK GOES ANOTHER ROUND. To Dan this is hilarious. He tosses the newspaper in the backseat and hands over the tape recorder. Nothing but the sound of a phone ringing on the tape and a garbled exchange between the Holiday Inn desk lady and Dan, who seems to be talking in a polite tone, obviously taken aback by the grandeur of the lobby and perhaps wanting to put his best foot forward . . . *If by chance there is a room available next to the Phish suites . . .*

"Let's get the hell out of Canada," I say, kicking the Jimmy into gear. We drive down the tall city corridors, dark and deserted. Eyes half-shut, Dan curses the Pita Put, promising revenge. As he falls asleep, he jolts awake for a second mumbling about "Sloth," how he just can't believe it—"*Sloth*"! With his seat tilted back, mouth open, Phish sticker pasted on his collared shirt, Dan falls into a deep sleep.

Driving at night in a foreign country is a strange experience, almost spooky. Even though it's only Canada, the highway seems to stretch across another planet. The sky is different, the street lamps are oddly shaped, somehow futuristic. On the horizon a band of white lights trace a bizarre pattern over the landscape.

The signs at the exits aren't at all helpful. Each sign announces the town's population, but doesn't tell you anything else. In America, you know exactly what you'll find: Wendy's, Dunkin' Donuts, Motel 6 at one exit, Bob's Big Boy, Days Inn, Texaco at the next. Here in Canada you just have to guess. Which I do, hoping to find a motel.

Driving around an industrial park a mile or so off some awful exit, I get pulled over by a cop.

"You been drinking tonight?" he says, peering into my window.

"No, sir." In the tilted-back passenger seat, Dan snores loudly with his mouth open. If he wakes up shouting about Sloth we're in for it. "My friend here . . . he, ah, has been drinking. He's had a rough night."

"I can smell it," the cop says. He looks at Dan—a terrible sight. "Where you coming from?"

"Toronto. Heading back to the States." I don't mention a word about Phish. He's probably never heard of them, but you never know—there could be some kind of bulletin out over the Canadian wire. "I'm looking for a hotel and can't seem to find one anywhere."

Squinting his eyes, he glances again at Dan and shines a flashlight in the back of the car. "Okay. Hotel's down the road."

We pull into the Best Western at four a.m. No vacancy? Screw it. I park right next to the building and crank my seat back. This is home, the Best Western. I can picture the inside of the room, with the Best Western list of TV channels on top of the set and the Best Western plastic cups wrapped in cellophane in the bathroom and the Best Western bathmats with the king's crown etched in the middle.

I sleep for an hour or so and wake up as the edge of the sky turns pink. After a half hour of driving, we're near the border.

"Wake up, Dan. We're coming to the border."

He doesn't budge. He's a very heavy sleeper who usually needs a shake.

"Dan! Get up! It's the border. Come on, you need to put your-self together."

He opens his eyes and immediately starts yelling, "Planet Hollywood! Planet Hollywood!" (Long story.)

"Stop it! Wake up! It's the border."

Dan sits up, adjusts his seat, and looks around through foggy eyes. "Wow," he says. "I was out."

"Fix your collar and cover up that aftershow sticker."

He buckles up for the second time of the trip.

"Listen," I say, "let's have a no-talking policy for the next few minutes. Until we're through."

"Don't worry, I'm—"

"Eh? No talking! Not a word until we're through."

I know we have nothing to worry about, nothing illegal in the car, but just the thought of standing beside the Jimmy in the Canadian dawn while someone searches the car and Dan tries to stand up straight—just the thought of it gives me chills.

We show the customs man some identification. He looks through the window at both of us. Dan smiles.

"Okay, guys," he says, waving us on.

Back in the U.S.A. just like that, listening to Dancin' Oldies on the radio. Dan turns up Marvin Gaye. *Oh mercy, mercy me . . . Things ain't what they used to be . . .*

"I *love* Motown," he says.

The rest areas along this route have been completely taken over by Phishheads, each one turned into a campground. Tents everywhere, sleeping bags covering every patch of grass. No one moves. An early-morning fog hovers over a McDonald's rest stop. A cop steps out of his his car and walks through the sleeping crowd, orders them to get moving, pack it up. Nobody stirs. A few people turn over in their sleeping bags.

Dan chats with a guy named Camel from New Jersey, doing the whole tour. He wears patch pants and like everyone else is very grubby. He spots Dan's aftershow sticker and examines it closely. "Hey, can you get me one of those?"

Camel camped here last night and now he's being hassled by
the state cop to move his gear and get back on the road, which
makes him mad.

"I hope I get into a wreck!" Camel says to the cop. "I'm too
tired to drive."

The dirtiness factor here is off the charts. I showered yesterday morning and feel like a slimeball. Some of these people
haven't showered probably for days. A few people wash up in the
McDonald's bathroom, but most don't even bother. It's like you
grow a second skin on the road, slippery, and after a while you
don't even notice. Just douse on the patchouli. I know this
woman back in Burlington who never uses shampoo. She says
that hair doesn't need shampoo, that it isn't natural. The scalp
produces oils that work just fine, apparently. She keeps her long
hair up in a bun and every time I see her I think, *What the hell is
in that bun?*

A lot of people here are staring at Dan, wondering about that
sticker on his shirt.

"Dude, you went backstage?" a guy in a floppy hat says.

"Sort of," Dan says. "It's the aftershow, you know."

"Wow. I don't think I could ever do that. I'd get back there and just be . . . I don't know . . . I wouldn't know what to say. I'd look at them and be like, 'Good show, guys. I gotta go.' " Floppy Hat's name is Nick. He lives in Chicago and works as a manager of Target. "This is paid vacation for me," he says. "Yeah, man, benefits. Twelve bucks an hour, not bad. I've worked there four years now. I was on tour earlier in the summer and then I had to go back to work for a week and now I'm back on tour getting paid to be here."

Nick didn't like Canada, either. "I'm glad to be out of that place. The driving, man, those yellow things flashing across the street. And the whole money thing with the silver and the gold in the middle, what's that about? I was at the Burger King throwing money at the guy. 'Take it, I don't know.' I told him, 'The only thing I like about your country is that you have a nineteen drinking age.' "

It occurs to me that one reason people go on tour is to trade stories. To have adventures. To have something to talk about other than just the daily workaday routines of life. I mean, it *is* an adventure. And there's something old-fashioned about it. We have nothing to do with computers out here, nothing to do with television, or the World News Tonight, or professional sports. We're out here on the highways, a gang of cowboys—road cowboys with rest areas for watering holes. We pull up in our dusty rides, step out stiff-legged from the journey, nod to one another, and talk about life on the road. Where else in American life can you find this? Is anyone else doing this, living with a cult on the road, traveling the nation's interstates, beating drums as they go?

A Race Against Boredom

July 21, Burgettstown, Pennsylvania

We check into the Red Roof Inn in Washington, Pennsylvania, at midday. The sun beats down on everything. The air is actually offensive. It makes you angry. And the town is a depressing place. Not really a town, more like a strip mall. No one outside on the street, no one walking around. Cars drive by with all windows rolled up, sealed against the day. People stare out at the dead town from Wendy's, unwrapping hamburgers.

Minutes after stepping into our motel room, Dan falls asleep. An interesting and disturbing fact about Dan: he's been in two different comas in his life. At sixteen, he was in a bad car accident and was gone for three and a half days. Then a few years later he drank too much vodka and fell headfirst into a rock. That one lasted a day.

When Dan sleeps he *really* sleeps, and my theory is it's related to the comas. I can scream at the top of my lungs in the Red Roof motel room and he won't so much as vary his breathing pattern. Which is doubly strange considering what Dan says about his ears: "My hearing is off the charts. Literally. It's been tested. You know—*meep meep meep*—higher pitch? Things you're not supposed to be able to hear? I can hear."

We join the rest of the town at Wendy's for a late lunch. What a crew here, staring out the windows silently. I guess the locals aren't too happy with their town, either. A couple of Phishheads walk in and the locals turn and gape. This happens everywhere: Phishheads roll into Small Town, U.S.A., and every jaw drops for a few seconds. *What in the all hell . . . ?* Sometimes a town gets

wind of the imminent arrival of thousands of Phish fans and they
prepare for the big day. It's a chance to (a) sit on lawn chairs and
watch the freaks roll in, and (b) make a lot of money. Rumors
start among shop owners when they hear that fifty thousand
Phishheads will be driving into town. "It's a crazy hippie bunch
chasing after a band," they must say at town meetings. "They're
called Phish. Spelled with a PH—Phish. And none of them eat
meat, so don't bother with burgers. And they like that fancy beer.
Microbrew or whatever. Won't drink Bud. Not one of them." So
every town you pull into has signs all over the place: WELCOME
PHISH PHANS! . . . PHRESH VEGGIE BURGERS! . . . MICROBREWS! Some
of them get carried away with the whole P-H thing, like it truly
is part of the language of this weirdo cult: HAVE A PHANTASTIC
TIME! . . . BY TWO GET A SECOND PHOR PHREE!

I talked to one lady, a pizza-joint waitress, who said she heard
that Phishheads don't like pizza. "So we stocked up on bagels
instead," she said.

The other thing that happens in Small Town, U.S.A., when
Phishheads roar into town, is that a group of rednecks inevitably
decide to defend their turf. They pile into pickup trucks and
cruise the town to watch the freak show. They make sure the
newcomers are aware of their presence. Last summer in Maine, a
group of buzz cuts patrolled Main Street—up and down, up and
down, waiting for the herds of fans to arrive. From a colorfully
painted school bus, the first Phishheads stepped out one by one,
dancing and skipping about, music tinkling out the windows. The
guys in the pickup revved their engines and drove by real slow,
eyeballing these wild-haired hippies, peering into the bus windows. After the second or third drive by, they peeled out, mark-
ing their Main Street with a long black streak, screeching
through town. The Phishheads watched them race by.

In this way the summer tour is completely different from the
other Phish tours—fall, holiday, spring—where the band plays
indoor arenas, usually in the downtown section of major cities.

The summer-tour open-air pavilions are for the most part in the
middle of nowhere. Within a short drive, usually, of a city, but
still you're talking about fairly depressed areas. In the colder
months, Phish books the biggest venues in the biggest cities, and
all their fans, bundled in raggedy sweaters, hang out on sidewalks
and huddle around lampposts. In Boston, they take over the
blocks outside the Fleet Center and set up vending areas in narrow alleyways. The Boston police force always sends out the
horses, which stand serenely, tails swishing, taking in the scene.
In New York, Phish books Madison Square Garden—the greatest
place anywhere to see Phish play, with the taxis and the people
and the lights and the energy of Manhattan all around. Outside
the Garden, Phishheads set up shop for the four-show run leading to New Year's Eve. On each of these afternoons, in the early
darkness, commuters with briefcases, their faces buried in jackets,
shuffle by MSG on their way home, puzzled. They glance at the
crowd, thinking, *My God, this sort of thing still exists? Where do
these people come from?*

The Wendy's scene here in western Pennsylvania is just too
depressing. I can't eat my food. I think after a while your body
shuts down rather than accept another fast-food meal. In fact, my
body appears to be breaking down—nose constantly running,
coughing every minute, a general sluggishness. I feel like I've
been beat up, kicked around. You can't eat healthy on the road,
not even at Wendy's, which has a salad bar. My salad is withered
and droopy and for some reason the whole thing is soggy even
though I haven't poured one drop of salad dressing. It's simply
impossible to find a healthy meal in a town like this, even with
the locals flipping veggie burgers for the hippie visitors. America's food is fried and fried some more and then slathered in
grease. I usually love this crap. Back at home I make the
rounds—Dunkin' Donuts, McDonald's, Denny's. I truly am a
regular at Denny's. But on the road, three times a day, I can't take

it. Nobody could, really. The band has their own caterers on the road. Once, for a show last summer—I was writing a newspaper story at the time—I was backstage briefly around dinnertime and you wouldn't believe the spread. You could find just about whatever you wanted to eat, and there must have been at least a hundred people back there with paper plates piled high. One woman stood behind a long table of fresh fruit, tossing strawberries and pineapples into a blender and pouring tall smoothies. You could order whatever combination you wanted. As far as I could tell, this was her only job. So of course the band doesn't have to worry about the fast-food problem. They don't have to worry about much, food-wise.* The time I was back there, Trey was playing with his kids, Fishman was zooming along on a golf cart, and Mike was walking around with a big green parrot on his shoulder, picking at the buffet table.

We hit the show on an empty stomach—the Star Lake Amphitheatre in Burgettstown, about twenty minutes from the Red Roof Inn. Our seats are pretty good—on the floor, a little bit to the right, maybe twenty rows back. Security isn't very strict tonight so all sorts of people have weaseled into our row, making it hard to dance or even just stand in place without getting bumped. In front of me, in my space, a miniature woman, dragging her miniature boyfriend with her, has somehow inserted herself and her little man in the sliver of air between me and the person in front of me. They're about five feet tall. They hold hands and sway to the music, pinning me against my chair. I bump him, but he doesn't take the hint. I'm not going to bump

---

*This of course wasn't always true. In a 1992 blurb in *The New Yorker*, Trey said: "I'll give you an average week. Let's say we play until two. We get to the hotel by four. We sleep exactly eight hours and get woken up by the maids at noon. We hobble out to the van. We try to find a Denny's. We eat breakfast, drive for four hours, and get out of the van just in time for a sound check. We sit backstage for two hours eating some kind of measly meal. Then we go onstage, play until two, get to the hotel by four."

her. They've slipped in like two little minnows and there's really nothing I can do about it. If I asked them to leave, then (a) I'd look like a dick, and (b) I'd have to shout in order to be heard over the music, make a big scene. And there's this general understanding at shows that you should be able to dance wherever you like. But you know, fuck that. Where's the Gestapo security when you need them?

The real problem, however, is to my left. This shirtless dude is dancing like a maniac, an obnoxious maniac with no regard for personal space. His arms are flying, whacking me, and occasionally he spins around helicopter-style, arms stretched like rotors, mowing down whatever's in his path. I try to give him a look, but his eyes are closed and he's smiling, which makes me even madder.

"This guy is terrible," I say to Dan. "He's ruining the show."

Dan leans over and looks down the row. He shakes his head.

And then the helicopter jerk lands on my foot, my bare foot.

"I'm gonna stand my ground," I say to Dan. I stand up tall, cross my arms, and stick out my left elbow. I make sure the bony part projects at just the right angle. Here comes Helicopter again, closing in, and this time he gets it right in the ribcage, my elbow, with a little twist timed just so. He crumples. A second later he looks at me, surprised, and I smile at him.

Farther down our row, on the other side of Dan, a giant guy, who Dan refers to as Goliath (we've seen him at past shows), dances with plenty of room around him, a nice clear space in an overcrowded row. I watch him for a second to see how he does it. He's a huge blond gorilla in overalls, very sweaty, and whenever someone wanders into his space, he fixes them a stare and shakes his big head.

The show itself isn't going too well. Phish is off tonight. Mike forgets the lyrics to one song and then another. Trey teases him about it between songs. "Mike forgot the words to that one," he tells the crowd. And now Mike looks angry. In the second set they play "Mike's Song" and "Simple" and "Weekapaug Groove," three Phish classics that collectively make up what's become known as "Mike's Groove."

"I bet it's cause Mike was pissed between sets," Dan says. "So, you know, they want to make him happy."

After the show, in the parking lot, a guy with squinty eyes and dreads walks up to Dan, smiling.

"Hey, man," he says, "how's it going?"

"Fine," Dan says.

"Hey, you look different than the last time I saw you."

"Yeah?"

"So what you been up to, man?"

"Not much," Dan says. "How about you?"

"Just chillin' like a villain."

They talk for a little while, and when he leaves I ask Dan, "Who was that?"

"I have no idea," he says.

On tour, people are always on the lookout for anyone they've met before. You try to keep up the contacts, no matter how tenuous, because you never know where it might lead—who will have an extra ticket, an extra joint, maybe some extra van room for a ride to the next show. As in any other part of life, it helps to know people.

Denny's, two a.m. McDonald's this morning, Wendy's for lunch, and now grilled cheese on rye at Denny's with the air conditioner turned up much too high. I shiver and cough.

"I think we should put a little bit of effort tomorrow into getting something healthy to eat," Dan says. He orders the Denny's Grand Slam—eggs, pancakes, bacon, sausage.

"Yeah, we should. My body needs some nutrition."

We don't say much else for the rest of the meal.

Photos of JFK Jr. and his missing plane on the cover of *USA Today*. What a terrible thing. I read or heard somewhere in the last day or two that JFK Jr. lived his life as "a race against boredom." It might have been his uncle Ted Kennedy who said it, though I'm not sure. I like that. I like the idea of living life this way. . . . At the start of this tour, I asked some Phishheads I met on the road, "Why do you do this? Why do you think so many people follow this band around?" I never really got a good answer, so I stopped asking. Mostly, people said they do it for the music and quickly trailed off into talking about something else. At some point I realized that it was a dumb question I was asking. Dumb because it's unanswerable. Why do you do this? Why do you do what you do? Because you do, that's why. For a million reasons—one of them being, perhaps, that the tour itself is a race against boredom. A race against the suburbs, nine-to-five, a race away from the persistent call of career and complacency, settling down and growing roots in a mortgaged yard. Who wants to grow roots when you can hit the road and roam the country? The tour, life on the tour, offers up the idea that life really can be full of surprise and adventure.

In the travel industry, adventure vacations have boomed in recent years. Climb mountains! Raft rivers! Bike deserts! It's the promise of real adventure, the promise of life away from the remote control. The Phish tour taps into the same thing—fear of dullness, of living a boring, colorless existence. Fear of death, even. Phish shows ultimately celebrate living in the moment. That's what rock and roll is: living in the here and now, forgetting for a few minutes that the clock is ticking for each one of us, every minute, and all we can do, really, is try to ignore that consuming fact and enjoy our surroundings while we can.

A Goddamn Impossible Way of Life

July 22, The Rock and Roll Hall of Fame and Museum, Cleveland

Listening to an oldies disco station on the way to the Rock and Roll Hall of Fame . . . *Burn baby burn . . . burn baby burn . . .* Dan particularly likes these dancin' oldies stations because the gravel-throated DJs often dive into Motown tunes.

"Al Green is smooth," Dan says, as the next song comes on. "Barry White is also smooth," he says a few minutes later.

Oldies stations have changed. It's not fifties doowop anymore or "Sixteen Candles." I can remember driving across country with my family as a kid and my dad would land on some oldies station and say, "Now *this* is good music." My brother and I would groan and put on our headphones, crank up the Guns N' Roses. "Boys, have you heard of Buddy Holly? You must have heard of Buddy Holly." Looking out the backseat window, I'd picture for a second or two my dad and mom at a 1950s prom dancing strangely to Buddy Holly. And now there's not much Buddy Holly left on American radio. You can still find him, occasionally, but it's not nearly as easy as it was even ten years ago. These days music from the seventies dominates the oldies stations, and a lot of forty-year-old women call up to make requests on the air. Even some songs from the eighties make it into the oldies rotations, particularly heavy metal ballads. Each metal band did a couple of sappy tunes—slow-dance material at the high school semiformal—and somehow the heavy metal ballads have survived longer than the headbanging football-locker-room songs.

Every single place we've been in America in the last few weeks has had an oldies station. Out in the country, where you don't pick up many stations at all, you can always tune in to *Slammin' Oldies* or *Dancin' Oldies* or *The Best of the Seventies*. Music from your youth of course reminds you of your youth—often in a very powerful, detailed way. This is why oldies stations are successful, the reason why people tune in to hear songs that came out twenty, thirty years ago. Shelved in the back of our minds we have a whole stash of memories, but we don't know precisely what's there. We forget that in some of these files stored away are exact bits of conversation, clear snapshots of an afternoon long ago, the sound of a certain girl's laugh, the smell of a particular car. A rock and roll song can access a file that's been closed for years. Whenever I hear John Cougar Mellencamp's "Hurts So Good," I remember that my friend gave me *American Fool* for my birthday in the sixth grade and that the lyric "Come on, baby, make it hurt so good" fascinated me in its dirtiness. I wasn't exactly sure what he meant by it, but I really liked it, and I remember now the feeling it produced in my stomach—a nervous excitement, an antsy desire to grow up as quickly as possible and find out what the hell Mellencamp was talking about.

A bit of new life in us today with no show to make tonight. No pressure to claim our seats by seven p.m. We drive three hours north to the Rock and Roll Hall of Fame in Cleveland, which opened a few years ago and now attracts more than a million visitors per year. We pull into a space next to a Phish-stickered car.

The building itself, a giant glass pyramid structure, sits on the shore of Lake Erie, a short walk from downtown Cleveland. The terrible sun reflects off the pyramid and shoots its beams around like lasers. This midwestern heat, it's simply unbelievable. I've never felt anything like it before. Never again will I complain about summer heat in New England. That's nothing. At least you can function outside, your brain still works properly. The Midwest is an oven. It wrecks you. The heat creeps into your eyes and ears and boils through your body. You can't think. Every part of your body sweats, even your shins. I sweat through three or four t-shirts a day—I'm talking about drenched t-shirts that I peel off and stick into a plastic bag in the back of the Jimmy. I drink gallons of fluids and never have to go to the bathroom.

Inside the glass pyramid it feels like an igloo. The Midwest survives on industrial-strength air conditioners that send nasty chills down your spine. Your entire system gets this shock dozens of times a day. Riding the escalators, we spot a few Phishheads and they spot us. Nods all around as we ride down and they ride up.

Larger-than-life photos of Mick Jagger and Keith Richards as young men, staring impishly at the camera. Wall-size photos of the Beatles, young and smart-alecky, on top of the world at twenty-five. No middle-aged shots of Mick or Keith in evidence. No wrinkles yet. Rock and roll as youth—a powerful image. And also a depressing image because how do you face your forties and fifties in rock and roll?

Rock and roll and youth are fiercely linked at the hip. The energy of rock and roll, the wildness of it, comes out of youth. Rock stars aren't made at forty-five. They're made at twenty-five, sprung onto stage, kids suddenly famous. A few years back, when the U.S. Postal Service decided to distribute an Elvis stamp, they had a couple of different images in mind—a young blue-suede-shoes Elvis or an older 1970s Vegasy Elvis. They weren't sure which one to go with, so they held a vote. Millions of people paid to vote. They bought a stamp and mailed in their vote. Most Americans don't even vote for government positions, and that's free. We turn out in pathetic numbers to vote for the people that make our laws. Yet millions of people were compelled to vote for a particular image of Elvis. Overwhelmingly, they voted for the youthful Elvis. Who wants to commemorate the pill-popping Elvis of later years, bloated and jowly, an embarrassing reminder of what he once was? If the stamp in question had been a presidential stamp—a young, bespectacled Harry S Truman or an older, bespectacled Harry S Truman—it wouldn't have mattered. Millions of people would not have paid to vote.

PHOTO COURTESY OF DOUGLASS M. TITUS

The dream of youth. Rock and roll serves up the dream of youth. And so does this museum. Only a handful of bands make it to the other side—make it to middle age playing their guitars, dignity intact. The few that do, that keep selling records, keep producing new material, keep drawing crowds, these small few become legends. The Rolling Stones still sell out stadiums. They always will. Mick is fifty-six and running around with super-models, siring kids all over the place, the pursed-lipped bad boy of rock and roll. The Grateful Dead made it into their fifties and were more popular than ever when Jerry Garcia died in 1995. There aren't many like these two. I can't think of any other band that has lasted thirty-plus years, growing in popularity as time goes by. Phish will survive. They will play to packed houses as long as they stay together. Unlike most successful bands, Phish hasn't had the fifteen minutes of fame. They've never had a moment in the spotlight. No hit song or hit video, which for the long haul is a good thing. They just keep building and building, a steady musical force feeding on the power and immediacy of live rock and roll.

VH1 runs a show called *Where Are They Now?* They track down former rock stars and find out what they're up to now that their time in the spotlight has passed. The most depressing one I've seen so far features this longhaired heavy metal dude in his forties who moved back in with his mom. I can't remember what band he was in during his heyday. After an impressive run in the early eighties, traveling the world, women screaming for him, he ends up a decade later with absolutely nothing. The run is over. He has no money left and no career prospects. He's starting a new band, and who can blame him? If rock and roll is what you know, why should you stop doing it? How can you stop doing it? Once you've heard the roar of a stadium crowd, or even a noisy club, how could you do anything else? In very few professions are you considered washed up in middle age. At least professional athletes can hang around the game as a coach or sportscaster and it's not considered a disgrace. But there's something quite pitiful about the rock star hanging on, making a comeback or hitting the road for a reunion tour, playing the state fairs. It is incredibly cruel that the aging rock star is considered pathetic. Desperate, we say. Sorry-ass. Disgraceful. Indecent, even. Isn't there something obscene about the Beach Boys taking the stage in their sixties, singing about California Girls? It makes you cringe to think of it. But what else is there for them to do? In a recent interview, Bob Dylan said he's addicted to the stage, addicted to performing. He's spent years and years on a kind of never-ending tour, and at the end of the day what keeps him going is the performance itself. Dylan's lucky. My guess is that many people in rock and roll develop this addiction and very few get to feed it, like Dylan, for thirty-five years.

Most of the mannequins here—dressed up as Madonna, Prince, Alice Cooper, etc.—have wide-open mouths, O-shaped. I've never seen open-mouthed mannequins before. They look perverse. Like blow-up dolls. I suppose the curators had it in mind to capture the singing thing, the musician in a full-throated chorus, but it doesn't work.

I head for the theater on the bottom floor, which runs two rock and roll documentaries. Both of them are excellent. The first film is a brief history of rock and roll's roots in the migration of blacks from the Deep South in the 1920s to Chicago, bringing the blues with them. A great shot of Leadbelly singing his classic "Good Night, Irene." Leadbelly was serving a life sentence for murder in Louisiana's Angola State Penitentiary when he wrote this song. The governor of Louisiana liked it so much he pardoned Leadbelly. Rock and roll born of outlaws, a tradition that carries on today, the rock star as outlaw: from Tommy Lee of Motley Crüe to Tupac Shakur to Axl Rose.

Watching this film, you get the sense that rock and roll was also born of travel, movement, migration. The most compelling image in the film is an old steam-engine locomotive churning along, going someplace, blues song in the background. We're not sure where the engine's going, but it's moving out, last call to get on board. The train whistles and chugs away, rumbling down the tracks to someplace new. The filmmaker returns to this shot again and again. At the end you're left with the feeling of rock and roll itself traveling somewhere, searching for something new. Rock and roll is always searching for something new and different, breaking new ground—whether it's Elvis in the fifties gyrating his hips on *Ed Sullivan*, Dylan in the sixties plugging in his electric guitar, David Bowie cross-dressing in the seventies, Madonna touching herself in the eighties, Limp Bizkit doing it all for the nookie in the nineties. It's not always exactly clear what the point is behind pushing the envelope. I mean, what's the point of Bowie dressing as a woman except that it's daring, challenging, outlawish? Rock and roll's trailblazers will always be considered outlaws by mainstream society, at least in their own time. *The Ed Sullivan Show* wouldn't permit its cameras to film Elvis below the waist. Now we smile fondly at such a notion. How could they be so innocent—so . . . well, charming? When Madonna started touching herself in her videos, eyeballing the camera ravenously, we were shocked. Is she *really*? My God, she *is*!

In the second film at the Hall of Fame, we see a bunch of interviews with rock stars, most of whom are now middle-aged, looking back on their careers. A couple of good nuggets:

Robbie Robertson: "It's a goddamn impossible way of life." He's talking about life for the musicians themselves, of course. But just *following* the musicians is impossible enough. I can't imagine doing this for years and years. Living in hotels, no matter how nice, traveling in buses, no matter how super-plush, is just too disorienting. It beats you up, the rootlessness. It kicks your ass. And that's not even taking into account the reckless partying. I recently saw a VH1 Rockumentary on Motley Crüe and it is truly amazing to me that those guys are still alive. I bet if you did a study on the average life span of a rock and roll star, it is significantly below the American average.

Keith Richards: "Everybody knows people who . . . you just have that feeling that they're not going to be, they're not going to be seventy years old ever. Not everybody makes it." It's clear that Keith is talking about himself here, in this bit of footage shot when he was a young man. He wasn't always a scary-looking dude. Not quite handsome with his crooked teeth, but not too bad, either. Keith didn't expect to make it this far—still on stage and approaching sixty, his face like it's been dragged through the wars.

Ozzy Osbourne: "The thing with it [the rock star's life], you do what you want. You don't have to go lift for some big fat baldy old fart, telling you to pack this box and stick it over there, you know." When I was a kid, a rumor started at school that Ozzy bit the heads off chickens at his concerts. Did anyone else hear this rumor? Was this a national thing, or was it just among my classmates? It terrified me at the time. Still today when I hear an Ozzy tune I think of him wild-eyed and bloody on stage.

And then Joe Strummer of The Clash: "Rock and roll reminds you, to put it in a nutshell, that it's fun to be alive. It's like when you watch a kid skipping down the street and everybody else on the street is worrying about their rents or whatever, and you see a kid skipping down the street, like dancing through puddles, and it reminds you that it's fun to be alive. I think rock and roll exists to deliver this truth."

He nails it, Strummer. The guy with the mohawk on The Clash albums, the fierce-looking dude who to me, at ten or eleven, might as well have been a murderer the way he looked—Strummer, in middle age, on camera, his stage years behind him, and he just nails it. I watch the film a second time to hear him talk.

More Strummer: "Pure rock and roll is when the past no longer exists, the future doesn't exist, and it's like a howling moment in the present when the band and the audience become as one and you just occupy a moment completely and fully."

This howling moment stuff is what becomes addictive. It's what you hope for at a Phish show. If you're lucky, it happens a few times a night: the music builds and builds, frenzied, out of control . . . and then the explosive release, the howling moment. It sounds quite sexual, of course. In a way it is. It doesn't make you horny, though. At least it doesn't make *me* horny. You feel . . . what? Happy. Thrilled. Excited. Pumped. You feel like you could dance forever. More than anything, it makes it fun to be alive.

We pull out of the Rock and Roll Hall of Fame with Billy Joel on the radio. Old-school Billy Joel, circa 1980.

How about a pair of pink sidewinders,
And a bright orange pair of pants?

The first album I ever owned—*Glass Houses*. My mom was concerned that it had curses. I *loved* that it had curses. On the cover: Joel in a leather jacket and blue jeans, rock in hand, about to chuck it at a glass house. Blue sky reflected in the glass. It looks like a cold day. Back cover: Joel in a loosely knotted tie staring through a broken window. His expression says, *I'm sorry, but what did you expect?* My babysitter bought the album for me on the recommendation of her boyfriend, a mustached dude who worked at the dry cleaner's and thought it was a cool record. I'd come home from school and crank it on my dad's record player, jump around the living room.

> Hot funk, cool punk, even if it's old junk
> It's still rock and roll to me

The album started with the crash of glass and then the first few notes of "You May Be Right." I'd place the needle on the very edge of the record, buying a few seconds to take my position in the middle of the living room. No one was home yet. Out the front window, the street was empty except for a few dogs . . .

> Friday night I crashed your party
> Saturday I said I'm sorry
> Sunday came and trashed me out again
> I was only having fun
> Wasn't hurting anyone
> And we all enjoyed the weekend for a change

Two o'clock in the afternoon, bookbag thrown on the floor, drinking Nestlé's chocolate milk and dancing to Billy Joel. I played it over and over again. I'm sure most people have some sort of memory like this. It put me in such a mood. I could do *anything*. I'd turn up my collar and check out my reflection in the full-length mirror on my mom's closet door. "Yeah, that's right, you can *dance*, mister."

Hit Me with Music

July 23, Columbus, Ohio

Poolside at the Motel 6 shortly after nine a.m. Earliest start to the day I've had in weeks. With no show last night and nowhere to travel, I was asleep by midnight, well before our three a.m. tour average.

Ninety degrees and the sun is barely off the horizon. My laptop's keyboard is damp in the sticky air. For now I have the pool to myself and a lounge chair cranked to sitting position. Soon, I'm sure, a few Phishheads will crawl out of their rooms in grimy bathing suits and splash around, though probably not until noon at the very earliest. The sun will drive me back into the room before then and I won't write a single word in there. Dan will wake up in an hour or so, grab the remote control, and flick the channels from underneath a cocoon of covers. The air conditioner blasts frigid air day and night, and you don't want any skin exposed. It's probably why I'm sick. I'll go back to the room in a few minutes, flop on the bed, wrap the covers tight, and won't move for hours. What a way to spend the days-—hanging out in dark motel rooms with the curtains drawn and the air conditioner clanking away, dirty clothes strewn on the floor. We'll both yell "No thank you!" to the maid's midday knock on the door, but she won't hear us over the roar of the AC, and she'll click open the door with her master key, take one surprised look inside at the two heads poking from the bedsheets, squinting at the new light, and quickly close the door.

It's an impossible lifestyle, Robbie Robertson of The Band said in that Rock and Roll Hall of Fame documentary. I keep hearing him saying that over and over again. I feel like I've aged five years in the last month—not a good thing, since I'm already twenty-seven. I honestly think I might be too old for this shit. If I was twenty-one maybe I'd have more energy, or more *something* . . . more fire. Every now and then on the road the question pops up: So what's your guess on the average age of fans on tour? The question came up a lot with Shack, who seemed even more distressed than me about hurtling towards thirty. The most common answer to the question was early twenties—although on particularly depressing days it seemed like the answer should be eighteen or nineteen. Shack and I both agreed, time and again, that we saw plenty of people in the thirtyish range.

A blonde woman walks across the parking lot wearing a bathing suit and a Motel 6 towel. (Unlike the Best Western's, the Motel 6 towels don't have an emblem and they aren't nearly as soft.) She tosses the towel on a lounge chair and dives in—a dangerous maneuver, since the pool is small and the transition from deep end to shallow end is quite abrupt. In the shallow end you can jump in and barely get your bathing suit wet. She's pretty. She smiles a lot and seems to really appreciate the pool water, skimming her fingers along the surface, watching the little wake of bubbles she leaves behind. A few minutes later a door opens across the parking lot and a bearded guy walks this way in a pair of cut-off khaki shorts, knee-length. No towel for him. When he swings open the black metal gate, the woman in the pool smiles even more and swims to the pool's edge. He sits there for a minute dangling his feet. Neither of them say anything, probably because I'm here on the lounge chair a few feet away, and you know how guys are when other guys are around—the last thing in the world you want to do is act all lovey-dovey. So he swims a few strokes and she dives around him like a dolphin, shooting between his legs as he stands there in the shallow end trying to fully open his eyes in the glittering sunlight. Then she comes up for air and wraps her legs around his waist and locks her hands behind his neck. She stays straddled for a minute or so, pressing her hips into him, rotating slightly. It's the first overtly sexual thing I've seen in weeks. It startles me. She arches her back and dips her hair in the water, her legs still vise-gripped around his torso. I watch them over the top of my computer screen. My bet is they just had sex minutes ago back in the room and this is the afterglow. I continue the pecking sound on my keyboard for fear of seeming creepy otherwise.

An hour later I jump in for a swim and end up talking with Derek, a tall guy kneeling in the shallow end. He's a Phishhead from Virginia who's bounced between a few community colleges and recently settled on geography as a major. He's on tour this summer with a few friends who've made thousands of bucks selling t-shirts on the road. "They were living large in Manhattan for the Jersey shows," Derek says. He describes the t-shirt and why it's such a hot seller, but I can't quite follow what he's saying, graphically.

Derek has been to sixty-three Phish shows. Sixty-three exactly. You'd be surprised how many people can tell you the precise number of Phish shows they've been to. "I'm addicted," Derek says. "My favorite song is 'Mike's Song.' When they start out with 'Mike's Song,' I'm just, you know, I'm *ready*."

Motel pools, I've decided, are the best places to meet Phishheads and gather information for the book. No one's going anywhere. Another good reporting zone: the Best Western lobby during the Free Continental Breakfast. It's not always smooth sailing in the lobby, however, because people eat in groups at small tables and the last thing you want to do is approach a whole table with a series of questions. In the pool, people usually swim alone, and if you time it right you can get them in the corner. With their arms stretched out along the edge, face pointed at the sun, it's fairly easy to get people talking. I've definitely done some of my best reportage in pools. Not that my interaction with Derek is all that interesting or full of quotable gems—it isn't really, even though I fire off what I think are potentially provocative questions—but at least we talk for a while, and at the end of it I feel like I'm *connecting* to people on tour. That I'm not just eavesdropping, like my brother said.

I tell Derek about the book project and he seems curious, sort of, even though he doesn't ask me any questions about it. Most people I meet, I don't mention the book. Sometimes I do if I talk with them for a while and develop some kind of mini-relationship. In that case I feel obligated to mention the book. But most people you meet on tour, you interact with for a couple of minutes and that's it. Move on. The problem with marching around announcing to everyone that you're a writer is that (a) people clam up or (b) they try to say something original and funny, which backfires. And plus, I don't like telling people I'm a writer. Hard to explain why, really. Partly because I hate giving up my anonymity. The last thing I want to be, bobbing around the Motel 6 pool, is the Writer Guy prying people for information. It's cowardly, but I tell myself that it's cowardliness with a purpose: better to eavesdrop and get honest bits of conversation here and there, rather than walking around all the time with a pencil behind my ear or a tape recorder in hand.

Dan shows up poolside. He's not much one for actually going *in* the pool. Rather, he likes to find a spot under the umbrella and stare off into space for a while, adjust to daylight. He's a slow mover before noon. This morning, however, Dan has a mission: margaritas.

The supermarket trip is a total failure: all tequila bottles, including Cuervo for chrissake, are 20 percent alcohol by volume, which after our third supermarket enrages Dan. He's as mad as I've seen him. He corners some poor red-aproned teenage clerk to ask him what the hell is going on.

One massive supermarket after another, with aisles as wide as streets, hundreds of yards long. The people and the carts way down at the other end by the meat section actually appear small. The cereal boxes are enormous. There's nothing like this on the East Coast. There's too much land out here. Too much space to fill. I'm talking about supermarkets the size of stadiums and parking lots like deserts—you can't see the end.

Poolside, with a genuine bottle of Cuervo Gold, Dan's mood improves. He downs two pint-sized margaritas and rattles the ice for the last few drops.

"Yeah," he says, "this is the life right here."

Dan truly loves life on the road. He loves everything about the journey. Back in Vermont he's always planning a trip—New Orleans for Jazz Fest, California to visit a friend, New York for a Phish show. He always has something in the works.

I ask him why he thinks people follow Phish.

"The music," he says. "And it's a wild party."

I ask him to elaborate.

"They do some crazy things at their concerts, just off-the-wall weird stuff you'd never expect. So you don't want to miss the next show, because what if they top that? Like you go to Halloween in Vegas, you see them do the Velvet Underground album, and then you *don't* go to Salt Lake and you *don't* see *Dark Side of the Moon* by Pink Floyd—that sucks."

There is a feeling on tour of what will these guys do next? And every serious fan has this thought: I need to be there for *that* show. Johnny Mac told me about what he missed last summer, on tour with his roommate. "We were in Burgettstown last summer," he said, "and we both missed 'Terrapin' for these really shitty reasons. We were both crushed because we were enormous Dead fans. And the next night, oh, we were devastated, just devastated. There's no way to communicate how awful we felt. The next night we get down there and they open up with 'Trenchtown Rock' and we were just amazed by this. Earlier this summer I had given Fishman this really wonderful soundboard disc that I had burned of this Marley show opening with this unbelievable 'Trenchtown Rock.' Fishman, when he ran away from home when he was a kid, had been to this Marley show and they opened with 'Trenchtown Rock'—you know, '*One good thing about music, when it hits you you feel no pain'*—and he said he just started bawling. It opened everything up for him.

"After missing 'Terrapin,' which was so heartbreaking, to have him the next night open up with that, it was the one thing that could've made it better, you know. We saw him after the show and he was like, 'I had to play that song. Of all the covers, that was the one I needed to hear.' I said, 'Oh, you have no idea how much I've needed to hear it.'"

Three p.m. and padding around the pool's deck barefoot with a margarita. This is about as good as it gets on tour. A perfect day for *USA Today* and a lounge chair. The big news in rock and roll this weekend is the thirtieth-anniversary Woodstock concert in upstate New York, where they are expecting a couple hundred thousand people. The question, of course, that comes up over and over is, What does this 1999 Woodstock have in common with the 1969 Woodstock? The consensus seems to be: not much. "It's a giant festival that has no meaning whatsoever," Fred Durst says in *USA Today*'s Woodstock preview story. Durst is the leader of Limp Bizkit, a rap-metal band—one of the hottest groups of the summer and a Saturday-night headliner at Woodstock.

Grinning and sunburned, gripping his red plastic cup, Dan is making the pool rounds. He can be quite social, a regular Mr. Chitchat when the mood strikes. He's carrying on with a group of Phishheads near the pool and seems to be having a grand old time.

He comes back with a report that he thinks I should include in the book:

"I was talking to them about the shows they've been to and this big guy with a mustache and a shaved head comes up and says to them, 'I was just talking with my son and we we're just trying to figure out, Are you guys hippies?' All conversation stopped, people stopped smiling, and they were just like, 'Ah . . . I don't know.' And then he says, 'Cause when I was your age, about 1969, people were dressed just like you guys with the

beards, and you know hippies were around and then gone for a couple of years and now I guess they're back.' "

"What did they say?"

"Nothing really. They just smiled politely."

The conversation apparently ended with the guy saying, "Phish? What the hell is Phish?"

The answer to that question—"Are you hippies?"—is of course no. We're talking about completely different generations, thirty years apart. I don't think Generation X has any kind of hope that we can make a real difference, that we can truly change the world for the better. The spirit isn't around. And it's certainly not in evidence on this tour.

Five-twenty p.m. Monster traffic jam outside the Polaris Amphitheatre in Columbus, Ohio. A lot of drug deals go down in traffic. The dealer gets in a car and you can see the exchange through the rear window. Plenty of cops along the side of the road, standing around directing traffic. Working alone, one cop with a bit of fire in the belly could collar ten people an hour, easily.

Nothing quite like the smell of patchouli and exhaust on a steamy highway. The sky has clouded over and the sun seems to have slipped under the gray horizon and melted into the black asphalt below us, blasting its ferocious heat upwards. The cars on the highway don't move. Earlier in the trip, Will advised me not to dawdle too much on traffic jams in the book—and that if I was going on and on about traffic jams, it wasn't a good sign for the book in general. He's probably right.

So, moving on . . . Dan claims to thoroughly enjoy life on tour, likes being in a new place each day. "You meet people from all over the place," he says. "You can be like, 'I got a buddy in northern Virginia, I got a buddy in western Pennsylvania.' You got freedom, you can go anywhere you want to. It's something different every day. You have no commitments at all. Your biggest commitment is to be in Columbus tomorrow night, and if you don't go to the show in Columbus you can still make Alpine Valley or Deer Creek. You're just out there, and that's good for anybody, no matter what you do. You're just cruising."

Often in these afternoon traffic jams I take out the cell phone and call Jill. She gets home from the hospital around five or six and goes for a run, so we talk while she's stretching or drinking water and I tell her about my day. It's hard to come up with much to say—"Well, we're heading to another show, and last night was fun"—but then I don't want to bring up last night because of the whole . . . I don't know, it just makes her suspicious, the late nights, and makes me feel guilty for really no reason at all. So we end up talking about not very much. She's coming out to Indiana tomorrow for a couple of days. I pick her up at the airport in the morning.

Tonight's show is a damn good one—one of the best of the tour. Lots of rain and thunder and lightning, which perhaps gives Phish a little extra energy. Towards the end of the show, Dan makes two new friends: Trish and Matt. Trish is a stripper who works at a club north of Columbus. She has long reddish-brown

hair and wears an extremely tight dress split up the side. Matt is
a factory worker who I think would like to be Trish's boyfriend,
but for now it's not clear what exactly their relationship is. This
is their first show. They have backstage passes, too. (Apparently
last night the Phish road crew stopped at Trish's club and, well,
they liked her enough to give her two tickets and aftershow
stickers.)

So now we're backstage at the aftershow with Trish and Matt,
drinking Rolling Rock from the bottle. It's a crowded room in a
wing off the Main Event stage. I think this is Ohio's version of a
VIP room, though it has the feel of a rec room—easy-to-clean
floors, fluorescent lights, plastic chairs. Stripper types are not a
regular part of the Phish backstage scene. No one else here looks
even remotely like Trish, who can't stop wiggling. Every part of
her body moves in a slow snaky motion, like she's trying to shed
her dress. And when you're hanging out with a stripper in this
crowd, you yourself definitely get looked at sideways as part of
the stripper party. No one else here knows that Trish is a stripper,
but she's definitely *something*, that much is clear. The aftershows
are generally full of attractive women, but attractive in a J. Crew
kind of a way. Even if their jeans are tattered, they look showered
and rosy-cheeked. When I ask Trish about what she does, she
says, "I travel around and get fucked up." She's a tremendous
curser, by the way, dropping the F-bomb all over the place in a
flat and bored-sounding tone. And she looks bored, too—tapping
her toe, pursing her lips, sticking her hip out to one side and then
the other, aggressively. She seems to expect something to *happen*. Like, is this a backstage party or what?

The wind and rain thrash the windows. In the darkness outside, you can just make out the yellow lights of eighteen-wheel-
ers parked in rear-stage bays. The trucks, I think, are Phish
equipment trucks. No sign yet of Trish's roadie crew. She seems
to be on the lookout.

We all leave together. Everyone notices when Trish leaves. Her
walk is, I don't know how to describe it . . . I didn't think people

in real life actually walked this way. We troop along next to her through the crowd and I feel sort of like a bodyguard, or like one of those guys in a celebrity's retinue who ends up blurry in the corner of a magazine photo. We duck inside the Jimmy to escape the rain. We sit there, the four of us, with not much to say. When the rain lets up, Trish and Matt leave and Dan and I sit on the Jimmy's back bumper drinking beer in a light drizzle. We talk to Phil, a grad student from Michigan, dressed head to toe in green rain gear. He's following Phish on a motorcycle, which he says is tough on the wet roads, but the great advantage is "you get to blast in and out of places."

"It's a Kawasaki," Phil says. "But it looks just like a Harley Fat Boy."

He asks us if we want to buy some mushrooms. I don't. Neither does Dan, seeing that he already gobbled some mushrooms a few hours ago. These mushrooms, Phil tells us, are extra-powerful due to his very own growing process, involving a fish tank, sterile lab gloves, Saran Wrap, and rubbing alcohol (which gives me the shivers, just thinking about it).

Phil gave up acid a few years ago, after a bad experience, and mostly sticks to mushrooms and Ecstasy.

"I've just been into Ecstasy, man, this tour. You gotta do Ecstasy. Have you done Ecstasy?"

"No."

"You gotta do it. I've been munching a lot of Ecstasy tonight."

"How much?"

"Tonight? Ah . . . three."

I tell him about my brownie experience, figuring he might have some insight about the whole incident. I go into the whole ordeal, and I don't think he's really following the story line, even though he's nodding his head and sipping his beer.

Dinner

July 24, Noblesville, Indiana

Said goodbye to Dan this morning in our dark Motel 6 room. He barely opened his eyes when I left. It was a sorry sight—tequila mix spilled on the rug, a half-drunk bottle of Cuervo beside his bed, blanket pulled up to his nose.

Now it's eight p.m. and I'm sitting in the first nice restaurant of the entire trip—an upscale Italian place in the middle of suburban Indiana. It's the first place in a month that's not a truck stop or a fast-food joint. It's expensive, but what the hell—Jill's here and she won't eat at Taco Bell. It's one of the few spots I've been on tour that isn't crawling with Phishheads. Big blond mid-westerners sit elbow to elbow around giant tables with tire-size plates. The men are thick-necked and brawny and I bet they all played football in college. I don't think there's a man in here under two hundred pounds. The women are pretty and smile a lot and wear a fair amount of makeup. The din of voices sounds all male.

It feels odd talking to Jill about the tour. Yesterday, sitting in traffic with people selling drugs and Dan gobbling mushrooms . . . well, it all seemed very normal, and now just talking about it seems strange and I feel almost criminal. It's weird, the distance that comes up between us when we are apart. When I picked Jill up at the airport today, it was almost like picking up a stranger. Everything was awkward. Walking through the terminal, I didn't know what to say and neither did she. We talked about this and that and we were friendly, but it was uncomfortable. The trip has not been the best thing for us. It's like the road, the highways, all the states I've been through, have piled up between us—this huge mountain of parking lots and amphitheaters and VW buses and Best Westerns, one on top of another, with me on one side and her on the other. I'm not saying everything was perfect before the tour started—it wasn't. But the tour has made it worse. Whoever said absence makes the heart grow fonder didn't get it right. Absence makes the heart uneasy and doubtful. Now, here in the restaurant, some of the ice between us has melted. We've both let our guard down a bit, but there's still a cloud, some fog, that we can't quite see through.

Back in Black

July 25, Noblesville, Indiana

USA *Today* has been running a half-page advertisement for the Personal Cooling System, $49. It's a U-shaped Star Trekky thing that clamps around your neck and blows cool air. It runs on batteries and only weighs ten ounces and comes equipped with aluminum cooling plates. The woman in the ad looks very refreshed and doesn't seem to mind the gizmo hooked on her neck. It may be a good investment.

In the Sahara Desert you can't survive more than a day without water, even if you're not doing anything. I bet survival rates in the Midwest today would be just as low, particularly in the vast concrete parking lots. If you stood out here on the black asphalt today, just stood still, I bet you wouldn't make it to sunset. I've never felt heat like this before. In the morning, Jill and I load up on food at the supermarket and head back to the hotel. We hit the pool and sit in the shade. I sit in the sun for a minute to dry off, but that's about it. On the other side of the pool a group of collegey guys in sunglasses watch Jill walk around the pool in her bikini.

The heat just takes over after a while and so we retreat to the room and watch MTV, which has devoted its weekend to covering Woodstock. Bad stuff happened there last night in Rome, New York. It started with the crowd throwing bottles on stage and quickly escalated into a riot. It looks like a war zone this morning with police in riot gear and garbage everywhere and roaming mobs of shirtless men. All the reporters are acting stunned and shocked. But is it really that surprising? A riot broke out somewhere in a crowd of two hundred thousand people with a lineup of Limp Bizkit and Kid Rock on stage. I'd be shocked this morning if everything had gone smoothly last night. Rock and roll has a nasty streak.

When I was in high school I played on a very good lacrosse team. We beat everyone. We ruled the league. Before game time, in the locker room, we had a ritual: turn off the lights and blast AC/DC. The locker room was a giant brick-and-mortar cave in an old building with exposed pipes, cement floors, and no windows. We laced up our cleats, slid on our pads, buckled our helmets, and then the captain walked over to the boom box and stuck in the tape. Someone else turned off the lights. It was so dark you couldn't even see the bars of your own face mask. No talking allowed. The music pumped through your whole body, echoed inside your helmet. Sometimes, for big games, we would all lie down on the cement floor, holding our sticks above us like battle axes. When the song ended our coach flicked on the lights. He ate up this AC/DC stuff. He once tacked a self-made poster beside the boom box with some sicko quote from Genghis Kahn, something about crushing the enemy and hearing the lamentations of the women. It was written in his own handwriting, the letters getting smaller towards the end to squeeze it all in. On the field, at the start of the game, AC/DC still boiling inside of us, we'd charge out full of fire and ready for battle. It's hard to express the hunger, the desire to inflict pain, that was in the air at the start of those games. I never really felt it myself, to be honest. I wanted desperately to feel it, the anger, the blood thirst. I never did. But I saw it in my teammates. I'm sure if you've played a violent sport—football, ice hockey, lacrosse—you know what I'm talking about. My point is, the music, the AC/DC routine, brought all of this out. Without AC/DC, we still would have been a fearsome team. With AC/DC, a few of us became ferocious—swinging sticks like warriors, slashing opponents, marching off to the penalty box snorting and satisfied.

It's not at all surprising to me that Limp Bizkit's brand of rap-metal could incite such a riot at Woodstock. Of course it could. Music is incredibly powerful. Is the music itself to blame? No. I think Fred Durst, Limp Bizkit's lead singer, was an idiot to say on stage "Fuck shit up," or whatever it was he said. That was irresponsible and dangerous. But rock and roll has always said "Fuck shit up." It's always been, at its heart, irresponsible and dangerous. And with a Saturday-night lineup of Rage Against the Machine, Korn, Kid Rock, and Limp Bizkit, is it really that surprising that a riot broke out? It's like getting all these lacrosse players cranked on AC/DC and sending them off to the field—some dudes are going to swing sticks at heads. There's really nothing to be done about it. You can't stop the Limp Bizkits of the industry. The music has a right to be played. Don't go to Limp Bizkit concerts, I guess. Because it could happen again. It will happen again.

We head to the Phish show late in the afternoon. I sit next to a guy named Darwin from Tennessee. It's his fiftieth show. "I'm all about Trey and that funky guitar," he says. Darwin and his friends, a whole row of them, are on mushrooms. One guy in the group, down the row a bit, starts scratching his legs before the show. *Really* scratching them. He starts looking around nervously. I get a wave of fear just watching this guy, thinking of the rising tide inside his mind, the building anxiety. He stands up, tears his shirt off, and starts dancing. The show hasn't started yet and he's really moving now. He's not dancing in a relaxed manner, either. More like dancing to keep from shaking. Anything to get out of his own mind. I can't watch him for more than a few seconds.

"I did the summer tour last year and it killed me," Darwin says.

"I know what you mean."

"I'm only doing a few shows this summer. This is our annual pilgrimage to Deer Creek. Last summer I spent a thousand bucks for the first six shows. I did it up. Bought some nasty nuggets in California and Oregon. Went to Vancouver, cookin' it, you know. I did it right. I love Vancouver."

In front of us, two longhairs grind pills into a white powder. They use credit cards, the grooved side, to grind the pills, hunched over in the dark. To our right, someone lights up a bowl. Down the aisle, the Tennessee mushroom crew shakes and twirls. Jill takes in the scene with a kind of fascination, the fascination doctors have with the really bad cases. She's of course learned all about these drugs in medical school, and my guess is she's thinking about what sort of narcotic reactions are occurring inside these people's bodies right now, on a cellular level. She's also voiced some concern about dealing with head trauma in a patient with thick dreadlocks. "It would be hard to clear the field," she said.

I feel pretty good as the show gets going. The one nice thing about this sticky air is that you never feel stiff, which makes for good dancing. By the end of show I'm dancing around like a maniac and Jill is slumped in her seat, worn out and ready for bed. I don't blame her. I thought I wasn't used to this lifestyle, but now I see that I'm not so bad. I'm just hitting my stride as midnight approaches. Phish ends the show with the Rolling Stones' "Loving Cup." Page on the grand piano . . . *Oh, what a beautiful buzz, what a beautiful buzz. . . .*

Outside the show, Phishheads roam around howling under the pale glow of tall parking-lot lights.

"I just could never do this," Jill says, walking back to the Jimmy.

"Yeah, it's not easy."

"I would never *want* to do this."

Tapers

July 26, Noblesville, Indiana

More trouble at Woodstock last night. Looting and arson and general mayhem. Trucks flipped over and set ablaze. Vending booths robbed and destroyed. Tents torn apart. An ATM mangled. The state police converged on the scene in full riot gear. What a disaster.* MTV's reporters fled the venue last night around midnight, their coverage turned into a series of dispatches from the Front. One man in the crowd died of a heart attack. Another broke his leg. It could have been much worse. Woodstock has, of course, made national news by now, and all the networks are flashing images of bonfires and mosh pits and naked people running wild. The New York State Police superintendent called the riot a "face-off" between his men and the crowd.

It's over now. Monday morning and the big cleanup begins. The concert promoters are blaming the riot on a few bad apples in a very large crowd. One of the event's organizers is actually telling reporters that there will be another Woodstock in the future. Even the mayor of Rome, New York, isn't ruling out the possibility of a return visit, provided certain measures are taken.

---

*The full extent of the riot didn't become clear until later, when four alleged rapes were reported. For a day or two, everyone in the media seemed to be talking about this terrible generation of American kids. Then a couple days later, a *New York Times* story pointed out that this kind of mayhem at rock festivals isn't a brand-new thing. It happened in 1969 at Altamont with the Rolling Stones and the Hell's Angels. Four people died there. Rapes were reported at the 1971 Celebration of Life festival in Louisiana, in 1982 at the Us Festival in California, and in 1994 at the 25th anniversary Woodstock.

I'd like to stay and flick channels all morning, from one Wood-stock report to the next, but there's a Free Continental Breakfast downstairs in the lobby and they close it down at eleven a.m. The problem in general with the Free Continental Breakfasts at motels everywhere is that no one monitors them. Occasionally, someone at the front desk will ask for your room number, but usually there's no motel employee in sight. Which means that food runs out. The first things to go are orange juice and cream cheese. I swear, every time I press the lever on the OJ machine a yellowish water comes out, and every time I toast a bagel there's no cream cheese packets left. The problem seems to be large fam-ilies that load up on the free food. I don't mean large as in num-bers. I'm talking large as in the actual physical size of the people in the family, kids included. Sometimes if I'm up early enough I'll see the families with plates piled high, huddled around the small round tables, going back for seconds and thirds. Usually, though, I don't catch them in the act, but instead wander into the breakfast area after they've already been through. If any donuts are left over, it'll be coconut or plain.

This morning I share a table with Dave from Chicago, who I met yesterday in the parking lot before the show. He works for a medical supply company. "I teach people how to hook up oxygen tanks and stuff like that," he says. "I tell my boss there are some days in the summer and fall when I just gotta go, I just gotta get out of here. He understands. He saw the Dead before. He knows what I'm talking about."

Dave plans to spend the day out by the pool and head to the show later in the afternoon. We both agree that motels are the way to do the tour. "I like the AC," Dave says. "I like the remote control. I like to live like a rock star on the road. I save up all my money, save up the cash, and go."

I tell him about the book and ask him what he thinks of the Phish phenomenon.

"I play the guitar, man. Actually I play just about everything—drums, bass, saxophone, whatever. But mostly guitar now. And the thing about these guys is they're incredible musicians. I mean, you're not going to find a better drummer than Fishman. And that style, man. Like he says, 'It's an ass on the seat with four limbs.' It's incredible. I don't know if you've been really up close to see him . . . but, man, you can go and see an eighty-piece orchestra and it's fine, you know, but these guys make you *move*. They make you dance. They make me dance so hard. I'll be dancing as hard as I can. I don't have anything left and they'll take it up a notch. They'll keep going."

I take Jill to the Indianapolis airport. She's due back in the hospital in Vermont tomorrow morning for six a.m. rounds. It's been a pretty grim weekend for her—the heat, the motels, the traffic, the Phishheads. She's not used to this sort of thing. Plus, she has a whole floor of patients back at the hospital that are always on her mind. She says things out of the blue like, "Gosh, I hope my cirrhosis lady doesn't have any upper GI bleeding."

I drive around downtown Indianapolis for a while. Not much to see really, and not many people around on a Monday afternoon. I've found this to be true of most cities on this tour—Syracuse, Pittsburgh, Cleveland—no one walking around in the middle of the day. Probably all hiding out in air-conditioned offices. It's depressing. One of the great things about cities is simply walking the sidewalks, seeing all the people.

It's very strange being alone on the tour all of a sudden. I don't really know what to do. I hate being alone in new places. It gives me the creeps. It's fine at home, being alone. In fact I like it. But once I'm out of my little comfort zone I'd much rather be with people I know. Otherwise I feel like an astronaut visiting the moon—it's just a big black void out there with nothing familiar.

I follow highway signs for the aquarium, for no reason really. I don't even particularly like aquariums. I go to the movies and see *Eyes Wide Shut*. In the middle of the day, it's me and a bunch of old men, maybe ten of us in there total, all scattered about the far ends of the theater.

Tonight is the last show of the summer tour and I end up somehow with a ticket in the tapers' section. At each show there is a section reserved for tapers, fans with high-tech equipment to record the shows. The tapers' section is 100 percent male tonight, as it usually is. In fact, there are far more men than women on tour in general. I would guess the ratio is five to one, maybe even higher. I've been thinking about this for a while, about this discrepancy, and the only thing I can come up with is that the tour is extremely hard, in many ways a kind of old-fashioned frontier kind of journey—logging mile after mile, pitching a tent at night under the stars, peeing in the woods. And men are drawn to this sort of adventure in greater numbers than women.*

The tapers are serious about what they do. They get here early and set up their gear—thousands of dollars' worth of gear. Each taper's ticket has an assigned seat, but the understanding among tapers is that you get to pick your own spot within the section if you arrive first. There are maybe fifty seats in here. My seat is in the front row, so that when I turn around I see a skyline of mikes perched atop silver and black poles. The guy sitting to my right, a nontaper, leans over and says, "Dude, you better not clap. These guys are serious." He wears sunglasses and talks slowly. "Don't talk too loud, either. They don't like that. They'll tell you *ssshhhh.*"

Tapers are the elder statesmen of the tour. Well into their thirties, most of them, and by far the most organized people on tour. People walk by the taper section and stare. No dreads in here, but a lot of ponytails and serious beards—beards that you can tell are at least ten years old. The tapers don't dance or shout or really show any visible signs of actually enjoying the show. It's more

---

*I talked to a friend about this later, about why men seem to be drawn to this sort of music more than women. He thinks that listening to music, disappearing for a while inside a long jam, is a form of therapy—a stress reliever. Women talk to each other all the time, work their problems out over coffee or whatever, whereas guys don't talk as much, don't get the release that talking brings. So they find it in other ways, like music.

like they're studying it. Each of them has a penlight to monitor their equipment, and a few of them don't even stand up for the show, preferring instead to sit, arms folded, and peer down at the floor and watch the tape spin.

The tapers, of course, provide a crucial service to the Phish community—they spread the music. In the early days, this was critical for the band. Without a record contract, without a hit song or a video, the only way to spread the word was to spin tapes for friends and pass them on. Some tapers have Web sites and list their catalog of shows. If you want a certain show, you send a tape with SASE and it arrives in the mail a week or so later—sometimes longer, depending on the popularity of a certain taper, e.g., someone who develops a reputation for having excellent sound quality.

Before the show starts, I end up chatting with a taper in my row, Antonio. He's a building contractor from California and has something like seven hundred bootlegs back at home. I ask him what it takes to get a good recording.

"There are a lot of hazards: beach balls, balloons, glow sticks. They can knock your mike around. Last year at the Fillmore this drunk guy fell over and brought down three mikes. It was a bad scene."

As the show gets rolling I take a beach ball in the head and Antonio springs up from his chair to guard his mike. Antonio is a great guy, answering all my questions between sets and not at all suspicious that I'm writing his comments down on the back of my ticket stub.

I reach into my pocket and pull out one of my aftershow stickers.

"Here, take this. I'm not going to need it tonight."

"Okay," he says. "Thanks. Thanks a lot." He seems quite happy about this and takes off to find his wife, who's up on the lawn somewhere. I consider giving him my other aftershow sticker, since I'm not going backstage by myself. Then I get thinking, Antonio's cool, but I don't know a thing about his wife.

What if she's, I don't know, strange, and they get stopped at the aftershow gate? Each sticker has these black initials in the corner, someone's signature, which means they might be able to trace the aftershow passes back to me. I have this vision of security cornering Antonio and his wife, demanding where they got the stickers.

"I don't know," Antonio might say, confused. "This guy. He's right over there. . . ."

I keep the sticker in my pocket and head out into the night.

I buy a veggie quesadilla and a Mountain Dew and sit on the back of the Jimmy for a while.

Main Street

July 28, Burlington, Vermont

My bus pulls into Burlington shortly after ten p.m. Jill is there waiting for me and we head into town for a beer. It's a warm Wednesday night with a nice breeze and the restaurants and bars have set up tables outside. What is it about coming home after a long trip? I feel like some internal compass has been wavering oddly for the last month, and now it has finally settled.

Lake Champlain is black and still. So are the mountains. We walk along Main Street, past a group of skateboarders, and we walk by Mr. Mike's pizza—empty now in midsummer without the college kids. We walk by Nectar's, the old stomping grounds for the boys. Outside Nectar's a longhaired man sits on a step, hunched over a drum, thumping away. There's live music every night of the week at Nectar's. One band after the next takes the stage and plays for small crowds. You see posters around town for this band or that, but not many people turn out at Nectar's anymore. It's a pretty grim scene most nights with the band on stage—people sip their drinks and look around and maybe one or two women in hiking boots will venture out on the dance floor. At the horseshoe-shaped bar a dozen or so middle-aged guys with mustaches and camo jackets check out any young women that wander in. If they do wander in, it's usually a mistake—they're looking for the dance club upstairs and went through the wrong door. They take one look around in their black stretch pants and scooch out quickly. Behind the stage, on the wall, are photos of Phish, which somehow makes everything with the poor band on stage wailing away even more pathetic. The decor in the restaurant, adjacent to the bar, is seventies time warp—very loungy, with red chairs, dim lights, everything tacky and old. In the men's room, there against the wall, are three old-fashioned down-to-the-floor American Standard urinals—the kind you just don't see anymore. Nectar's is also one of the last places in Burlington where there is truly nothing healthy on the menu. For two bucks you get a plate of gravy fries, which is just about the best food in the world any time past midnight.

We walk past Nectar's and cut through City Park. When I first moved to Burlington three years ago, I drove up from Boston alone and the first thing I did was sit in City Park for half an hour, waiting for Jill. She said we'd meet by the fountain. It was late August, and the entire park was swarming with Phishheads. They were everywhere, hundreds of them, hanging around, lying on the grass, smoking butts, beating drums, walking dogs. The night before, Phish had ended their summer tour across the lake in upstate New York, and afterwards there was nowhere to go. No show until the fall tour, so why not head over to Burlington for a while? I remember sitting there at the fountain in City Park and thinking, My god, I've never been to a place like this before. What the hell is going on here? A part of me also knew, immediately, that I would like Burlington. I was very wary about moving to Vermont, but something about the town felt right, the lake and the mountains and particularly this dreadlocked crew. It all felt right. I'm not sure why, exactly. Thinking back on it now, I realize that at twenty-four I had no idea what I was going to do with my life. (In the next couple years I would have five or six different jobs.) Somehow moving to a town full of young people kicking around a hackey sack was far more reassuring to me than a town full of cell phones and suits. This is going to be just fine, I thought, sitting at the fountain.

Tonight City Park is deserted. We head into a bar and find a table out on the patio. I spot a few friends across the bar and they spot me. We wave but don't get up from the table, and neither do they. Which is good, because I don't feel like talking about the trip at all. I'd much rather sit here and sip my Guinness with Jill's hand on my knee.